THIS BOOK BELONGS TO
THE MOM OF

_____

52
DEVOTIONS
FOR CAT
LADIES

BroadStreet
PUBLISHING

BroadStreet Publishing Group LLC
Savage, Minnesota, USA
Broadstreetpublishing.com

52 DEVOTIONS FOR CAT LADIES

978-1-4245-5915-2 (hardcover)
978-1-4245-5916-9 (ebook)

Devotional entries composed by Michelle Cox, Sylvia Schroeder, Lori Brown, Linda Gilden, and Edie Melson.

Design by Chris Garborg | garborgdesign.com
Editorial services by Michelle Winger | literallyprecise.com

Printed in China.

19 20 21 22 23 24 25 7 6 5 4 3 2 1

INTRODUCTION

All of us search for a special friend who will love us, spend time with us, make us laugh, and be our daily companion. For many people, that special friend comes in the form of a cat who steals their heart... and takes over their life!

Yes, cats can be finicky. Some have pretty big attitudes. They can be stand-offish at times, and they are geniuses at making messes. Still, those balls of fur bring endless joy.

We spend fun-filled hours playing with our cats, laughing as their eyes flick back and forth and their tails twitch wildly as they are tempted by a piece of yarn. We curl up with them on our laps, listening to their contented purrs.

Despite their reputation for being finicky, cats are quick to sense when we're upset. At times, they provide comfort when they notice our tears, rubbing up against us and staying close by.

Cats also give us spiritual and life lessons, and that's what you'll discover in this book. Each chapter contains a devotion, a prayer, a Bible verse, a question for reflection, and a fun fact about cats.

Curl up with your favorite kitty and spend time reading about the God-moments we uncover when hanging out with our feline friends.

IS THAT FOR ME?

The LORD came and stood, calling as at other times, "Samuel! Samuel!" And Samuel said, "Speak, for your servant hears."

1 SAMUEL 3:10 ESV

The minute I answered the phone, I knew the customer was annoyed. He was so angry I was surprised smoke wasn't coming through the receiver. "Look, lady, I've left two or three messages on your answering machine and asked someone to call me back. Don't you want my business?"

Several customers had called recently saying they'd left messages and nobody had returned their calls. I was puzzled. Maybe our machine was malfunctioning, or perhaps our sons had listened to the messages without saving them.

It remained a mystery until one day when I was polishing the furniture in the office. I heard a thud and turned around to see that our cat had jumped onto my husband's desk.

She stood there, her tail swishing back and forth like a symphony conductor's wand, then she inched across the desk, her eyes fixed on the flashing red light on the answering machine.

I watched as she extended her paw and pushed the play button next to the flashing light. She waited until my recorded greeting completed, and then as the messages began playing, she sprawled on the desk and listened to them. Once they ended, she jumped up and stalked from the room.

I giggled as I imagined the office door sign, "No Cats Allowed During Business Hours." I was ready the next time an irate customer phoned. "Sir, I'm sorry. The cat listened to your message and she must not have hit the save button."

I wonder how many times God has sent a message to us and we let distractions in our lives keep us from hearing his voice. Like young Samuel in the Bible, we should be waiting whenever God wants to speak to us. What if—just like our cat secretary—we'd listen, soaking in every word, until God completes the message he wants us to hear?

It would be such a shame to have the God of the universe stop by to tell us something, and we miss out on the wise counsel and words of love he has for us.

Father, sometimes I don't listen to your messages in the way that I should. Life and busyness get in the way. Give me ears that hear and a spirit that's attuned to you. Help me to hear your gentle whispers and to take your messages to heart. You are such a big God and it still boggles my mind that you want to talk to me. Remind me of what's really important each day, and help me to share your messages of hope, grace, mercy, and love with those who need to hear about them.

PAWS TO THINK

What can young Samuel in the Bible teach us about listening for God's voice?

DID YOU KNOW

Cats have over twenty muscles that control their ears.

GET ME OUT

The Lord is near to all who call upon Him,
to all who call upon Him in truth.

Psalm 145:18 NKJV

My three little boys looked at me with tear-stained faces. "Mama, you've got to do something!" As I glanced up at the tree where they were staring, I realized we might have a problem. A very big problem. One that I didn't have a clue how to fix.

I walked out to the yard. When I got there, I heard a pitiful "Meoooow!" coming from the tree. From my new vantage point, I realized the situation was even worse than I'd thought. Our gray tabby was on a branch about fifty feet up. Thankfully, my sons hadn't attempted to climb the tree to rescue her, but somehow I suspected they thought *I* should.

My husband set up our tallest ladder and tried to coax Fluffy into coming down to where he could reach her. When that didn't work, I handed him a can of tuna, hoping that the aroma would lure the cat, but no go. The tears flowed in earnest from the pint-sized audience. The frantic meows continued.

We'd done everything we knew to do, but one thing was evident—that cat was stuck.

Maybe some of you can relate. Not to being stuck in a tree, but to being stuck by your circumstances. By situations where you can't see any solution. Where desperation overwhelms you and hopelessness brings tears to your eyes. Maybe you've tried all you knew to do.

The starting point to becoming unstuck begins with what we did with our sons that afternoon when Fluffy was stuck in the tree. We prayed, telling God we didn't know what to do, and asking him to get their beloved kitty safely from the tree. Soon after that, Fluffy gathered the courage to climb down from her lofty perch.

God promises that he is near us if we'll just call upon him. In 1 Corinthians 10:13, he says that he will make the way of escape. There's hope, sweet friends. You can take heart because God answers prayer and help is on the way.

Father, I'm stuck today and I feel like there's no way out, like there's no solution to my problems. My heart is so heavy. I've tried everything I know to do to fix the situation, but nothing is getting any better. I realize now where I went wrong. I should have turned it over to you from the beginning. I should have prayed instead of whining and fretting. Today I place my problems in your oh-so-capable hands. Work out what is best for me and give me peace while I wait until the answer arrives.

PAWS TO THINK

Why is it that we so often try to fix our problems instead of placing them in God's hands?

DID YOU KNOW

A cat can't climb head-first down a tree because every claw on a cat's paw points the same way. To get down from a tree, a cat must back down.

READY TO POUNCE

Be sober, be vigilant; because your adversary the devil walks about like a roaring lion, seeking whom he may devour.

1 PETER 5:8 NKJV

I watched our cat from my kitchen window. From the way he was hunched over, I could tell he was doing something, but I wasn't close enough to see what was happening. I eased outside and quietly worked my way over to where he was in the yard... and then I wished I hadn't.

As I neared our cat, I realized that he was playing with a mouse. The mouse would try to run away, and the cat would let him take a step or two. Then a paw would shoot out and pounce on the mouse's tail so he couldn't escape.

The paw would lift again, giving the mouse freedom. The cat would let him go a short distance, and then he'd pounce again.

I sat a safe distance away and watched. That cat played with that mouse for a long time. Pounce. Release. Pounce. Trap him again. I watched the mouse grow weary. I didn't stay around long enough to see how the game of cat and mouse ended, but I suspect I know what happened.

Our lives are much like that of the mouse in my yard. Our adversary, Satan, lies in wait to pounce on us. He loves warfare and making our lives difficult especially when we're doing big things for God or trying to serve him with all our hearts.

Satan loves to trap us in our circumstances. Look at what he did to Job. His oxen and donkeys were stolen, and his farmhands were killed. Fire burned up his sheep and shepherds. His camels were stolen, and his servants were killed. And then the worst news of all, Job's children died when a powerful wind caused their house to collapse on them.

As Job learned, *nothing* can happen to us that God doesn't allow, and those difficult situations gave Job a closeness to God he'd never have had otherwise. Don't let Satan defeat you today from accomplishing the tasks God has called you to do. Satan will never win when he's up against the one who is in control of us and our circumstances.

God, sometimes I feel like my life is a constant stream of warfare. It seems I can't catch my breath from one difficult circumstance before another one arrives. I try so hard to live for you. That's the desire of my heart. I want to accomplish the purpose that you have for me to fulfill, but I'll admit that I'm weary in the journey. Please encourage my heart. Remind me that you have the power to defeat all of Satan's attacks. Use these situations to draw me closer to you and help me to learn what you want me to from these moments.

PAWS TO THINK

What can we learn from how Job
responded to his circumstances
and how can we apply that to our lives?

DID YOU KNOW

*A house cat's genome is 95.6 percent tiger,
and they share many behaviors with their jungle
ancestors. These behaviors include prey play,
prey stalking, and pouncing.*

BE STILL

Be still, and know that I am God.

PSALM 46:10 NKJV

I finally understood what my grandmother meant by "meet yourself coming and going." Some days, my schedule was so busy that I felt bad about taking time for lunch. I'd begun waking up with a stress headache. Those headaches made me re-evaluate my priorities, and I realized I had lost my morning quiet time.

Before, my routine involved spending a portion of every morning reading my Bible and praying. Now, I'm not a morning person or especially dedicated. I'm not a person who can voluntarily wake up at 5:00. I'm a late-night person, so my mornings start slowly, usually around 8:00.

As I got busier, I started the day so far behind I would skimp on my time with God. It sounds awful to admit, but it's true. The farther behind I got, the less time I spent with God—and the less time I spent with God, the farther behind I got. It took me a while to see the connection, and

I didn't discover it on my own. I got it from Emily Dickinson—my cat.

Emily has an unusual routine. Every afternoon, if I let her, she spends at least thirty minutes hanging out in my lap. I can be watching TV, knitting, or sitting at the computer, and up she hops. She stretches out, cradled in my arms, and rests. She is completely at ease. Sometimes, she'd fall to the ground if I didn't support her. She is completely unconcerned about any danger, knowing that I will keep her safe.

As God's children, we need that time of rest with him. We need to curl up in his arms, away from the trials of the day. He is always there, waiting for us, offering comfort and love.

Dear Lord, I'm in a familiar struggle. I've taken on too much, and I'm too busy. When will I ever learn? All this stress is taking a toll on me. I need you more than ever, but I have no time to spend with you. Please take over my schedule and fix it so it lines up with your priorities. Before I get into this situation again, step in and get my attention.

PAWS TO THINK

How do you make sure God
has top priority in your schedule?

DID YOU KNOW

*A cat has 230 bones in its body. A human has
206. A cat has no collarbone, so it can fit
through any opening the size of its head.*

I CHOOSE YOU

You are a chosen generation, a royal priesthood, a holy nation,
His own special people, that you may proclaim the praises
of Him who called you out of darkness into His marvelous light.

1 PETER 2:9 NKJV

My three sons were masters of the pitiful eyes. I think every parent will know what I'm talking about. It's that expression our children give us when they really want something—when they pull out every element of sweetness in their bodies, their pleading little faces almost impossible to resist.

I always called those expressions their "puppy dog eyes," but I saw them just as often when it came to an adorable kitten. I mean, what could be any cuter than a fluffy kitten purring loudly as it rubs its head against a child with a love-struck expression?

This mom must confess that it was often my fault that we got in these predicaments. I should have known better than to take three little boys to walk through an animal shelter or a pet adoption station just to look. Within a few moments of seeing the first few cats, they'd already found one, two, or three that they wanted. (I might have been guilty of that as well.)

By the time we'd walked through the shelter, they wanted to take all of them home with us to join the menagerie we already had there. "But, Mama! They don't have a home or anyone to love them!" How was I to resist those tear-filled eyes and sad faces?

As any responsible parent knows, we couldn't take them all even though, if we'll admit it, we big kids would often like to do just that.

I'm so glad that God doesn't have to do leave any of us behind. He opens the cages of sin and shame that hold us captive, and he says, "I choose you, and you, and you. I want to take all of you home with me. I'll pay the price. You can live with me, and I'll love you forever. All you have to do is accept my invitation."

God, if I'm honest, there have been so many times when I've felt unloved and unwanted. I've felt like those kittens begging someone to care, to show them kindness and affection. And then you walked by my life, reached out with a nail-scarred hand, and chose me. It boggles my mind that you want me to be part of your family. For always. Thank you for that security and for wanting me. Help me to tell others who are searching for love about you. Your doors are always open, and your welcome mat is always out.

PAWS TO THINK

How does it make you feel to know that the God who made the universe chose you?

DID YOU KNOW

It's estimated that 78 million dogs and 85.8 million cats are owned in the United States.

A HAIRCUT

Take up the full armor of God, so that you will be able to resist
in the evil day, and having done everything, to stand firm.

EPHESIANS 6:13 NASB

What's all that red stuff all over the stairs?" my husband asked. Paul had just arrived home from work a few moments before. I didn't know what he was talking about. Pregnant with our second child, I'd had a rough day of nausea, and while our four-year-old son, Jeremy, played on the floor in our family room, I'd stretched out on the couch for a few minutes to see if I'd feel better. Evidently, I'd unexpectedly fallen asleep for a few minutes, and Jeremy was no longer playing beside me.

He'd caused plenty of messes in the past. Jeremy took his scissors and cut the blooms off my poinsettias. He found the bottle of baby powder that I'd bought for when his new sibling arrived, and he discovered that if he squeezed the bottle, powder would come out in a giant poof of white. Let's just say there wasn't much left for the baby. Every time I vacuumed that room for the next couple of months, I smelled baby powder.

None of that explained the red stuff on the stairs. And then I saw the cat—who'd once sported ginger-colored fur—and I gasped. I asked Jeremy what happened and with an angelic face he said, "I sat on the stairs and petted the cat until he went to sleep. And then I gave him a shave and a haircut."

That poor cat was bald. Even his whiskers were gone. It took months for his fur to grow back. He'd gone to sleep and let down his guard, and now he bore the scars for those moments.

Friends, we often do the same thing. We don't pay attention to the things that will harm us spiritually, or we hang around in the wrong places, leaving us vulnerable. We must keep our guard up so the devil doesn't slip into our lives to defeat us. In Ephesians chapter six, God tells us to put on a helmet of salvation and a shield of faith, and to spend time in prayer and in his Word. Those things will equip us to withstand whatever comes our way. Just like that bald cat, none of us want to bear the scars of bad decisions.

Father, I often make bad decisions. I don't want to, but I do. Help me to remember that there are consequences to my actions, and that those consequences often impact those I love as well. Keep me from the wrong friends. Keep me from those who will draw me away from you. I don't want to go to sleep on the job spiritually. Instead, keep me alert for anything that would harm my testimony or my relationship with you. Help me to spend time in my Bible and in prayer, and to put on your armor so I can stand strong for you.

PAWS TO THINK

Why is it so important for us to stay alert spiritually and to put on the armor of God?

DID YOU KNOW

The whiskers on a cat's nose are generally about as long as the cat is wide. This helps cats figure out how wide an opening is and whether or not they will fit through it.

DON'T FEED THE STRAY

In everything I showed you that by working hard in this manner you must help the weak and remember the words of the Lord Jesus, that He Himself said, "It is more blessed to give than to receive."

ACTS 20:35 NASB

A beat-up white head appeared at the glass at our kitchen door. Nicks of fur had disappeared from numerous fights, leaving scars behind, even on his nose. The massive cat looked like he'd mostly been on the losing end of those fights. Add in that he had one blue eye and one green eye, and it's for sure he wouldn't have won any cat beauty pageants.

But whenever there are little boys and anything with fur, a quick friendship usually begins. When he got home from work that night, my husband cautioned our sons, "Don't feed that stray cat. I know we want to be nice to him, but if he starts eating here, he'll never leave, and we already have enough animals as it is."

Days went by and that ugly white cat kept hanging around. Just to make sure, I asked the boys if they'd been sneaking and feeding the cat. They replied that they'd pet-ted him but hadn't put any food out.

Then I made a discovery. One that busted my husband as I tiptoed outside to our deck and caught him in the act of feeding the cat. "Don't feed him, huh?" I said.

With a sheepish look, he replied, "He looked so hungry. I just had to give him something to eat." Long story short, it seemed we did have room for one more pet, and Igbert became an official much-loved member of our family.

Just as my husband showed kindness to the stray that showed up at our house, God has been so gracious and kind to us, and yet we sometimes act as if he's a well-kept secret instead of telling folks how he loves us so much that he gave his life for us.

What if instead of turning our backs on others we went and sought them out instead? There's always room for one more in God's family. There are so many people all around us who are hungry for what we have, who are looking for love. Let's invite them to become an official member of God's family because his welcome mat is always out.

Father, I'm so grateful that someone cared enough to tell me the greatest story ever told— the story of how you gave your life for mine. When I came to you, you didn't hesitate to welcome me. I discovered your door is always open and that you not only accepted me, but you considered me a beloved member of your family. Help me to be faithful about telling others about your love. Help me to look at others, especially outcasts, and to see them as you see them. Give me a heart of compassion and help me to remember that there's always room for one more.

PAWS TO THINK

Why are we sometimes hesitant
to tell others about Jesus?

DID YOU KNOW

Kittens become socialized by interacting with people, being held, spoken to, and played with from an early age.

UNEXPECTED

Bear with one another and, if anyone has a complaint against another, forgive each other; just as the Lord has forgiven you, so you also must forgive.

COLOSSIANS 3:13 NRSV

A number of years ago, I heard the story of a woman who settled in for a long night of sleep. She pulled the warm covers up, nestled her head into the pillow, and in mere moments, she was getting the rest her body needed. Then something happened that woke her from that deep sleep and made her scream in the dark.

Karen had a bookcase headboard on her bed. It was a wonderful place to tuck her necessities and whatever book she was reading before she went to sleep. Karen loved it and her cat did as well. Most nights would find him curled on the top, purring loudly as he went to sleep.

But on this particular night, he was in such a deep sleep that when he rolled over, he fell off the top of the book-case, landing on Karen's face. The startled cat dug his claws in trying to get his balance. The startled Karen woke to the unexpected sensation of sharp claws digging into her face. It was a traumatic time for both. Karen laughs about it now, but it wasn't funny when it happened.

Life is often the same way. We're going along just fine, and then someone digs their claws into our hearts, wounding us in a way that we never expected. Maybe it's someone's actions that hurt us. Or maybe it's the words they said that took root in our souls. Sometimes, like that cat who fell from the shelf, they didn't mean to hurt us.

Sometimes our first response is to get back at people for hurting us. But that's not the way God wants us to respond. The best way is to pray about our attitudes, and yes, to even pray for the person who hurt us. Becoming bitter always hurts us more than the other person. We're wise to forgive (even when it's not warranted) and to let God take care of the situation. When we handle it that way, we won't ever look back with regrets.

Father, it's hard when somebody hurts me, especially when it's someone I loved and trusted. I don't want to have a bitter or unforgiving spirit, but it's easy to do that. Help me to seek comfort in your Word and point out the messages I need to hear. Help me to have the right attitude and keep me from being the one who leaves claw marks on someone else's heart. Help me to ask for forgiveness when warranted and to grant forgiveness even when it isn't deserved. Thank you for forgiving me and granting me mercy and grace on so many occasions.

PAWS TO THINK

Why is it often hard to forgive? Is there someone you need to forgive today?

DID YOU KNOW

The claws on the cat's back paws aren't as sharp as the claws on the front paws because the claws in the back don't retract, and, consequently, become worn.

MERRY CHRISTMESS

The steps of a good man are ordered by the LORD,
And He delights in his way.
Though he fall, he shall not be utterly cast down;
For the LORD upholds him with His hand.

PSALM 37:23-24 NKJV

Fluffy had been fascinated with our Christmas décor since the first box came out of our storage closet. She sniffed around the boxes before we opened them. When we unwrapped the ornaments to decorate the tree and one of my sons dropped one, Fluffy took off like a world-class hockey player, batting the ornament across the floor with one paw and then another before we finally rescued it.

Our gray ball of fur loved sleeping under the Christmas tree. She looked like another accessory curled up there in the soft glow of the lights. However, Fluffy's main fascination was with the Christmas tree. I'd already scolded her several times for batting the ornaments on the lower branches with her paws. The scoldings didn't seem to make much difference since she kept playing with them.

Then something happened that disturbed the tranquil stillness of our family room as we enjoyed the decorations. Fluffy decided to climb the Christmas tree. That's what cats do in the wild, so she must have thought we'd brought a piece of the forest inside for her.

Ornaments went flying everywhere. Garland dangled from tree branches like broken power lines on a snowy day. I screamed, "No!" as I jumped from my chair. My husband and sons ran to the tree to remove the cat, but she panicked and kept jumping from limb to limb.

Yes, that cat made a giant mess. But don't we often do the same thing? As we run from the one who loves us and wants the best for us?

Just as we forgave Fluffy for her tree-climbing experience, God forgives us, granting us undeserved mercy and grace, showing us love when it isn't warranted. If we'll stop and truly think about it, isn't that what Christmas is all about? A God who came as a baby in a humble stable and then grew up and hung on a tree for us. He did this willingly, even though our lives were often big messes, because he loved us enough to give his life for ours. He turns our Christmess into a blessed and wonderful Christmas.

God, I often make a mess of things. I mean to do well and then I seem to do just the opposite. Thank you for your patience with me. I'm so grateful for your undeserved mercy and forgiveness. I don't want to make a mess of serving you, so please give me wisdom and guidance as I go through each day. Remind me to share you with others, telling them you can take our messed-up lives and turn them into gleaming lights in a dark world. Help my life to shine for you each day.

PAWS TO THINK

What are some times you've messed up and seen God's mercy?

DID YOU KNOW

Climbing trees is good for a cat's health. It improves their strength and flexibility and can also add a key defense skill to their list of abilities.

FRiVOLOUS PURRSUiTS

"You will seek the LORD your God, and you will find him
if you search after him with all your heart and soul."

DEUTERONOMY 4:29 NRSV

We knew the Christmas gift we bought for our sons would bring them pleasure, but we had no idea just how much fun they'd have using the gift in a completely unexpected way. We certainly didn't expect the hours of laughter it would bring to the whole family.

One of the Christmas wishes from our sons was for a race track with a remote control. Their squeals of excitement when they opened the package made it worth every penny we'd spent. The boys had so much fun playing with that track.

But they unexpectedly had to share their new toy. It seems our cat thought this was her own personal race track. We laughed at Fluffy as she tried to catch the cars. She'd lurk under a bridge, tail twitching, eyes intent on the car as it raced around the track, a furry paw reaching out to swipe it as it sped by.

Just as she was about to catch it, the boys would adjust the speed, making it zoom past too quickly for Fluffy to catch it. Or they'd make it go really slow as Fluffy watched and waited, and then they'd speed it up right before that chubby cat pounced. It provided hours of entertainment for the whole family, but Fluffy was engaged in a frivolous pursuit that wouldn't gain her anything.

We often do the same thing. We pursue senseless things like wealth, fame, designer clothes and handbags, and countless other items that won't matter for eternity. What if, like that cat chasing those race cars with such intent, we chased after God? What if we pursued him because we wanted to be with him? What if we prayed more and spent time in his Word? What if we focused on eternal things like reaching souls for God, pleasing him, and fulfilling the plans he has for our lives?

Let's determine today that as we race through life, we'll spend our days seeking God with our whole hearts.

Father, I often race after frivolous things, but in the grand scheme of life, those things don't really matter. Help me to chase after you with passion. Help me to seek you, to want to know your heart, and to take great delight in pleasing you. Remind me of what's important and help me focus on those things each day. Help my family and others to look at me and see a woman who's pursuing Jesus each day. I'm so grateful for your promise that if we seek you, we will find you.

PAWS TO THINK

What steps can you take to seek God more each day?

DID YOU KNOW

Female cats are typically right-pawed while male cats are typically left-pawed.

DON'T MESS WITH ME

The Lord will fight for you, and you shall hold your peace.

EXODUS 14:14 NKJV

Our cat, Martin, looked mighty cozy as he slept in the warm sunshine on our deck. I'll admit to being a little jealous that day because I would have loved to squeeze a nap in as well, but I knew that wouldn't happen. As I continued to watch that sleepy cat from my window, something unexpected occurred.

Martin awakened from his nap, but he didn't stretch lazily in the sunshine like he usually did. No, on this day, he jolted awake because he wasn't alone. A cat I'd never seen before had joined Martin on the deck, and it only took about two seconds to realize that the normally sweet Martin wasn't giving the stray a warm welcome.

Martin jumped up, and his back arched. The hair on his tail burred up, and he hissed in a threatening manner. When that didn't deter the interloper, Martin gave a hair-raising howl that was meant to scare off the new intruder.

Evidently the message wasn't delivered in the manner Martin intended because the visiting cat kept inching closer and closer. Martin's howls and hisses intensified, but the unwanted visitor kept advancing until the two cats were nose to nose.

That stray was delivering a message to Martin. "I'm not afraid of you because I know you're not going to do anything but make a lot of noise."

Satan often scares us like that as he makes threats against us, but we don't have to be afraid of him. I love the story in the book of Job where it tells how Satan tested Job. Satan wasn't allowed to do anything to Job without going through God first.

That gives us such confidence as we take our stand against the enemy. Just as the stray delivered that message to Martin, we can say, "I'm not afraid of you because I know the one who is truly in charge, and he fights my battles for me."

God, there have been many times when Satan has sent attacks against me. At times, he's messed up my relationships with those I love. Some days the warfare with him has been intense, and if I'm honest, there have been many occasions when I've been afraid or lost hope. Thank you for the reminder that you are in charge and that nothing can happen to me unless you allow it. Help me to learn from those times. Thank you for the confidence it gives me to know that you are in control and that you will fight my battles for me.

PAWS TO THINK

How does it make you feel to know that God is in charge of anything that happens to you?

DID YOU KNOW

A hissing cat should not be taken lightly. It's a warning that more aggressive behavior, such as biting or scratching, is coming if you don't give the cat some space.

GOD SEES

"The Lord sees not as man sees: man looks on the outward
appearance, but the Lord looks on the heart."

1 Samuel 16:7 esv

In my child's eyes, all our barn cats looked the same.
Short-haired, semi-wild, and tiger striped, their job as
exterminators kept them outside in both heat and cold,
rain or snow. One day my dad brought home Pierre. He
changed everything.

Only a French name seemed appropriate for such a
long-haired beauty. His white was so pure it disappeared in
the snow. His black patches so perfect they were invisible
in the dark night. His hair so long it waved in the breezy
Kansas wind.

Pierre liked to lounge, groom, and eat from a can. He
had no desire to catch mice or vermin. His flowing locks
were soon matted and full of briars. He wasn't hardy in the
cold and suffered in the heat. He really was meant to sit at
the fire and live a privileged city life. The farm didn't suit

Pierre, and Pierre didn't suit the farm. One day he simply disappeared.

When God instructed Samuel to go to Jesse's household and anoint one of his sons as king, there seemed to be a number of fine possibilities to pick from. Seven of Jesse's sons were there. Tall and handsome Eliab passed by first. *Surely, this is the next king*, Samuel thought.

All of the brothers passed in front of Samuel, but with each the Lord said, "Not that one." David, the youngest and least likely was tending sheep. When he stood before Samuel, the Lord said, "Arise, anoint him, for this is he."

We often judge by what's on the outside. God sees what is on the inside.

King David, once a shepherd boy, became the most famous king in Israel's history and a forerunner of the Messiah. God saw what no one else did. He still does.

Father, help me to remember today that you are looking into my heart. Forgive me for often judging people by what I see on the outside. Help me to resist comparisons. Help me remember what is important to you. Teach me to see people as you see them, and to value others as you do. Thank you for seeing me as I really am. Mold my heart to you alone. Fill me with your Spirit, so my actions this day reflect a heart that loves you above all else.

PAWS TO THINK

What do you notice first about a person, and why do you think that might be? What do you think God notices about you?

DID YOU KNOW

Barn cats can save money for farmers.

GOING AFTER TREASURE

"Store up for yourselves treasures in heaven, where moths and vermin do not destroy, and where thieves do not break in and steal. For where your treasure is, there your heart will be also."

MATTHEW 6:20-21 NIV

I don't know how Adrian, our cat, managed to not choke or hang himself when he soared directly into the bank window, but he made it look like a stately arrival to claim the treasures of an entire village.

Adrian, a pale cat with Siamese blue eyes, loved to bask in the morning sunshine against the warm surface of our tile terrace. We lived in a quaint little German village, directly above a bank. Because the balcony had stairs to the street below, we kept Adrian on a leash.

One soft spring day, the bank opened a tiny square window below us. As Adrian sat on the wide ledge, he heard voices below. His ears pivoted like tiny satellite dishes, searching for the sounds. His alert eyes strained over the edge. I saw him rise off his haunches, but before I could get to him, he leaped.

His collar and leash still on, I feared the worst. I ran out the door and down the terrace steps. An empty collar hung broken at the end of a swinging leash. I stood under the bank window, unsure what to do. Unmistakable sounds of chaos came from inside. "Hello?" I called.

After a few minutes, a shaken Adrian was passed through the window into my arms.

Jesus wants us to be treasure-hunters, but his definition of treasure may not match ours. When Jesus told his disciples to store up treasures in heaven, he wasn't talking about a bank-load of money. He meant true and lasting value. He wants us to understand that while riches aren't bad in themselves, they won't endure. No earthly wealth can compare with what God has planned for us.

Sometimes, I look to things or possessions for happiness. A new dress might make me smile, or a necklace might spark up an outfit. Jesus wants us to remember he is our treasure.

Father, thank you for loving and caring for me. I'm sorry I often look at the world to make me happy, when you want me to be satisfied with the treasure of yourself. Thank you for supplying what I need each day. Remind me that the things that count last forever. I want to cherish the things you do. I want my heart to treasure you more than anything this world can give me. When I forget and chase empty riches, would you remind me of what is really valuable? You are all I need.

PAWS TO THINK

What are some things that distract you from heavenly treasures?

DID YOU KNOW

At around six weeks old, kittens can successfully correct their balance during a fall and consistently land on their feet.

I'D RATHER BE HOME

Just as our bodies have many parts and each part has a special
function, so it is with Christ's body. We are many parts of one body,
and we all belong to each other.

ROMANS 12:4-5 NLT

Ellie sensed our transfer coming. She meowed at my feet
and kept so close our bodies tripped and tangled. When
she jumped onto my lap, her nose stretched to mine, test-
ing, questioning me. When I pulled out the boxes, Ellie sat
down on top of them and wouldn't budge.

International life made pet ownership tricky. Ellie
needed a place to live for three months. We couldn't afford
three months in a pet hotel, nor could we bring her with us
because there was no place to keep her stateside.

Ellie loved roaming the Italian town where we lived,
and almost everyone knew her. Welcomed into homes as
a guest, she spent hours lounging with the neighbors. Her
whiskers always bore traces of spaghetti sauce when she
came home.

Ellie was comfortable where she was. I hated the

thought of uprooting her to a strange place. Then I realized I might not need to. This was Ellie's home. Was it possible she might prefer to stay where she was even without us?

Ellie had always believed she belonged to the entire community, but could she really? Neighbors all around agreed to do exactly what they were already doing—loving, feeding, and caring for Ellie when she came to visit. We left enough food to feed an army of cats. A door into the garage gave shelter. Could our home still be hers?

After three months, we turned again into our Italian driveway. Ellie sat at the door, a few pounds heavier, ready to welcome us home.

We can feel uprooted and unsure of our place in the world. With Christ, we always have a place of belonging. We are part of his body, the church. We are members of a community meant to encourage and help each other.

In the book of Romans, Paul reminds us that just as physical bodies have different parts for different tasks, the body of Christ does too. We build up one another, and together we can accomplish more. Paul tells us we belong to each other even if we span the globe.

Father, I feel insecure today, uprooted and discouraged. Please be with me and help me to feel your presence. Remind me I am not abandoned. Give me a loving and caring spirit for others who are struggling. I have peace and assurance that my real home is with you. Help me share this truth with others who need to hear it. May I encourage my brothers and sisters in Christ and learn their needs. Thank you for your body of believers. Teach us to work together in harmony.

PAWS TO THINK

What can you do to help a neighbor
and show that you care?

DID YOU KNOW

*Some three hundred thousand feral cats live
in tourist spots in Rome, such as the Coliseum,
Forum, and Torre Argentina. They were officially
named part of the city's "bio-heritage."*

SCAREDY-CAT

Whenever I am afraid, I will trust in You.
In God (I will praise His word),
In God I have put my trust; I will not fear.
What can flesh do to me?

PSALM 56:3-4 NKJV

Nike could outrun us all. White kitty boots looked like sneakers against his golden fur, but speed combined with clumsiness landed him in all kinds of trouble. He shattered vases and destroyed food. Nike's greatest problem wasn't how he ran, but why. Nike was a big scaredy-cat.

Our apartment had a spiral stairway that led to a family room below the main floor. Nike had learned the art of sliding on our tile floors. It was hilarious until the tiny creature dropped straight past the spiral stair, down to the bottom floor. His little legs pawed frantically, and tiny cat claws scratched the air for traction. With only eight lives left, he never went close to those steps again.

Whenever the rest of the family gathered at the fireplace below to watch a movie or play a game, Nike sat at the top and meowed for us to carry him down. He never forgot that fall, and he never conquered his fear.

We can be scaredy-cats too. Fear paralyzes us. We forget that nothing is too big for God. He is the one we can trust when we are afraid.

In the Old Testament, David fought or fled for his life more than once. Fear caused David to pen the words in today's verse.

We think of David as a giant-slayer, a great warrior, and a fearless fighter. David had a lot to be afraid about, however, and he openly admitted his fear in many of the psalms. Everyone faces fear at some time. What we do with it demonstrates faith.

Psalm 56 is a song declaring David's trust in a praiseworthy God. King Saul was out to kill him, so David and his men hid in a cave. Even he felt like a scaredy-cat at times. No doubt his heart raced and his stomach knotted, but he knew where to take his fears. He believed God could conquer them, and he ran to the right place.

Father, I'm really afraid at times. I don't feel courageous or strong. You understood David when he felt that way, so I know you also understand me. Remind me that whenever I am afraid, I can trust in you. I praise you, because your Word teaches me how to trust you in every situation. Thank you for being my giant-slayer and taking care of everything that comes my way. Please take my fears and turn them into praise.

PAWS TO THINK

Where do you run when you are afraid?
Why?

DID YOU KNOW

Cats are afraid of cucumbers.

ALL ALONE

He Himself has said, "I will never leave you nor forsake you."

HEBREWS 13:5 NKJV

Our cat, Mitzy, glided into the room, her question mark tail held high. Heavy with a bellyful of kittens, she sniffed at an open suitcase on the floor. Gingerly, she lifted one foot, then moved in with all four paws. Lowering herself carefully, she settled her stomach against the tan lining. "You're not leaving me now, are you?" her green eyes pleaded.

"Mitzy girl," I sighed. "If you could just have those babies before we go!"

Boxes, luggage, piles of clothes, and the insistent needs of our four children made a chaotic house. Friends offered to keep Mitzy while we were away. I felt awful leaving her. She was about to give birth in a strange place with people she didn't know.

The following morning, I searched everywhere for Mitzy. Finally, I found her tucked in a box in a dark closet corner, two mewing balls of fur next to her.

Two days later, I carried Mitzy and her babies into a friend's house. Nervous and protective, she stayed in the box the entire time. When I put it down, Mitzy stretched her long neck and looked about. Fear and bewilderment glittered in her almond-shaped eyes. Why would someone she trusted leave her?

Have you ever felt like that? When events spiral out of control and you don't know what to do, you can feel abandoned. Situations are tougher. Confusion fogs your thoughts.

We sometimes feel like the disciples, their boat tossed from wave to wave in a storm. In their fear, they forgot that the Creator of the winds and waves was in their midst, asleep.

"Save us, Lord!" they cried. "We are perishing!"

Jesus had a question for them, and it's one for us, too. "Why are you so afraid?" With only his words, Jesus stilled the mighty winds and waters. No matter what circumstances we encounter, Jesus is there with his power.

I talked softly to Mitzy, petting her until some of the nervousness left. She relaxed into the box with her babies, knowing she was in good hands.

Jesus, sometimes I think I'm the only one that has certain problems. I feel alone. Today, remind me that I'm not. You are by my side. You will never abandon me. Please take the worries of my mind and the sadness in my heart. Help me to trust you no matter how I feel or how things look. Take control of every situation, so your will is done for your glory. Thank you for the comfort of your constant presence.

PAWS TO THINK

What makes you feel abandoned?
What changes that feeling?

DID YOU KNOW

The world's largest litter of domestic cats was born in 1970. A Burmese/Siamese in the UK gave birth to nineteen kittens, four of which were stillborn.

BLOCKING THE LIGHT

"You are the light of the world. A city set on a hill cannot be hidden. Nor do people light a lamp and put it under a basket, but on a stand, and it gives light to all in the house. In the same way, let your light shine before others, so that they may see your good works and give glory to your Father who is in heaven."

MATTHEW 5:14-16 ESV

An almost imperceptible meow followed us all day. Like a whispering conscience, we heard it when we parked at the grocery store. Throughout our shopping stops, a ghostly meow followed. My parents exchanged puzzled frowns.

"Do you hear it too?" Mom asked. I nodded. My thirteen-year-old imagination was crackling. Goosebumps prickled my arms. What in the world could it be?

When we parked again in front of our farmhouse, I crawled out of the back seat to figure out the phenomenon. I circled our '68 Chevy Caprice. When I crossed the front, a white-tipped paw reached toward me through the grille of the hidden headlights.

Behind the grating that covered the front of our car

were headlamps that opened and shut. Somehow, our cat climbed in when they were open and got stuck there when they closed. She had taken quite a ride around town, semi-protected and entirely concealed.

A cat in the headlight of a car would most definitely block its light. A covered light can't shine. It reminds me of a passage from the Sermon on the Mount. This discourse found in Matthew 5-7 is one of Jesus' best-known teachings. "You are the light of the world," Jesus told his disciples.

Jesus came to be the light of our world, but in these words, he impresses on us the honor and responsibility of shining as his lights. A light under a bushel—or a blocked headlight—can't produce the glow it should. It has little impact. Its purpose is thwarted.

When sin blocks our light, it's difficult for others to see Jesus. If we remove whatever shrouds our radiance, we can illuminate the darkness around us. In fact, we shine brighter in the blackest night.

Jesus wants us to reflect his brilliance, so everyone might come to know the true light of the world. Does your light shine unhindered today?

Dear Jesus, I confess there are things in my life that block your light. I don't want anything between us. Please show me how I can clear the path, so I reflect your pure light. Forgive me for sin that shrouds your light and makes it hard for people to see you living through me. You, Father, are the only true light of the world. I want to see your glory shine in my life and then spill your light to others around me. Keep me from allowing anything to get in the way of your radiance. Thank you for lighting my path today.

PAWS TO THINK

What things block your light
from shining brightly?

DID YOU KNOW

Cats do not meow to other cats. Meows are reserved for communicating with humans!

A GUILTY CONSCIENCE

The aim of such instruction is love that comes from a pure heart,
a good conscience, and sincere faith.

1 Timothy 1:5 nrsv

I stared at the mutilated piece of raw meat at our cat's feet. Newly married, my husband and I counted anniversaries by days and weeks. I'd splurged on steak to celebrate a new milestone. After dumping grocery bags on the kitchen counter, I turned to see our beautiful gray cat on her haunches, a bit of prime beef hanging from her teeth. Schnooks fled to hide under our bed. I planted my face on the floor, peering under the bedspread. Her eyes glistened from the farthest corner.

"You bad, bad cat. You come out from there!" I shouted. My rant ended abruptly at a knock on our apartment door. Two grim men stood in dark suits and somber ties. They whipped out badges.

"FBI, ma'am. May we come in?"

I let them in, feeling disadvantaged and oddly guilty. I'd been on a warpath with a feline. I was still angry and defensive. Schnooks stayed hidden under our bed, cowering—more likely triumphant.

"Do you know this woman?" They thrust a picture at me.

"No."

They scrutinized my face. "Our records say she lived here until July."

"That's impossible. We've lived here since June," I responded, feeling like a criminal.

"She resided here in Apartment 10-B, according to our records," one black-suited man said.

Relief washed over me. "This is Apartment 10-C."

The Apostle Paul understood the importance of a guilt-free conscience in the context of faith. He encouraged young Timothy to reject actions or beliefs of evil intent, which cloud our consciences. A good conscience is obtained by following God's Word. While our consciences are not infallible, they can be a good indicator of obedience. Scripture instructs and guides us to truth and purity, and Jesus leads us to freedom.

After a few more questions, the FBI men turned to leave. They walked around a beautiful gray and white cat blocking their path, serenely grooming off traces of raw meat.

Dear Father, I have guilt inside of me. Please, show me if I have sinned against you. I don't want anything to come between us. You paid the debt of my sin on the cross, and I thank you for salvation. Forgive me when I disobey your Word. Remind me that you forgive. In Christ, I am free from the guilt of sin. Take my shame and remorse and turn them into pure thoughts and actions. Help my trust in your salvation to grow. Teach me to love you, so I desire to please you in everything I do.

PAWS TO THINK

Why do we sometimes feel guilty
for mistakes even when no sin
is actually committed?

DID YOU KNOW

*In tigers and tabbies, the middle of the tongue
is covered in backward-pointing spines to break
off and grip meat.*

SPACE

When hard pressed, I cried to the LORD;
he brought me into a spacious place.
The LORD is with me; I will not be afraid.
What can mere mortals do to me?

PSALM 118:5-6 NIV

Space is relative. It changes with context, culture, and perception. Our family's tiny apartment shrunk with the arrival of one crazy kitten. No one passing by on the quiet street outside could possibly imagine the constricted frenzy inside.

My daughter nicknamed him the Cat from the Abyss. He had flaming orange fur, kaleidoscopic green-blue eyes, and the uncanny ability of careening around the apartment without touching the floor. He raced the perimeters of our narrow living-dining room. He leaped from the back of the couch to the end table, then onto the armchair, piano, dining chair, bookcase, and back to the couch. He picked up speed until watchers felt dizzy, trapped in tightening circles.

We all experience the disorientation of going around in circles. Days offer a confusion of circumstances that are uprooting and unpredictable. Life's bewildering cycle makes us want to step off, slow down, and regain our footing. The world continues to revolve, and everything flies by faster and faster. Perhaps that is how the author of Psalm 118 felt.

Distressed by dangers, threatened by enemies, and uncertain of outcomes, the psalmist was squeezed by life's vortex. He needed space to breathe. He needed a stable place to plant his feet. He cried to God, was brought to a spacious place. As if he'd taken a deep breath, he concludes that he no longer needs to be afraid. He went to the source of security and settled his unbalance with truth.

When we are hard-pressed and feel we are spinning faster and faster—like the Cat from the Abyss—there is a place of spaciousness. God waits to bring us there.

Father, life is crazy! I'm going in circles. Show me the spacious place the psalmist found. Help me to trust you, giving you all the thoughts that swirl in my mind, and the feelings that bind my heart into a tight ball. I want to give all of it to you. Please, put them into the order that is best. Bring my feet to a stable spot, so I can stand firm in the truth of God's Word. Let me experience the spacious place of your Spirit in my life and remember your presence. I give you the crazy circles of my life.

PAWS TO THiNK

In your life, what makes you feel
like you are spinning in circles?
How can God help?

DiD YOU KNOW

*Easy listening, classical, or instrumental
music is likely to soothe a kitten's nerves,
much like it calms humans.*

DROWNING IN TROUBLE

Save me, O God, for the waters have come up to my neck.
I sink in the miry depths, where there is no foothold.
I have come into the deep waters; the floods engulf me.

PSALM 69: 1-2 NIV

Napping like a pampered diva on my sleeping bag, our cat Tux barely cracked an eye when I attached his leash to the tent pole. I slid through the canvas flap and zipped it shut. We thought we would be gone a few minutes, but we had no idea a tornado was about to hit.

For real—a tornado! As soon as we arrived at the camp facilities, we ran for cover. Shower houses turned into storm shelters, harboring frightened campers. Outside, the massive storm unleashed its fury.

After the worst passed, we climbed back into our car. We inched our way back to our campsite, our headlights revealing a branch-strewn road. Lightning split the black sky, and we saw our tent, crumpled at the edge of the lake. We hurriedly slid down the embankment and waded into the shallow water.

A faint meow came from inside the canvas. Tux was up to his neck in water. Once freed, I put his wet, shaking body inside my jacket, zipped him against me, and headed for the safety of the car. We toweled him off and wrapped him in a blanket. Tux spent the rest of the night drawing in our warmth, finally sleeping in our arms.

There are times we are engulfed with trouble, as David illustrates in Psalm 69:1. His enemies sought to kill him, and he felt he was drowning in waters of suffering. David faced deep difficulties that challenged him physically, mentally, and spiritually. He pleaded for deliverance, for his feet to find solid ground from the mire of the overflowing floodwaters of affliction. He acknowledged his weak grip and how close he felt to being swept away.

In his infinite mercy, God heard David's cry. He hears ours too. When desperation rises, he is there to save. He reaches into our murky situations and pulls us into the safety of his arms. Tremors vanish in the warmth of his care.

Dear Jesus, sometimes I get overwhelmed. Sorrow and trouble pull me into mire I can't escape. I need you desperately. Save me from drowning! Reach down and pull me into your embrace. Hold me next to your heart. Show me how to rest in your care. Banish my fear and replace it with calm trust. May I depend on you to get me through the situations of life that overtake me. I trust you, Jesus, in every moment.

PAWS TO THINK

What makes you feel overwhelmed?

DID YOU KNOW

Turkish Van cats are nicknamed "swimming cats" for their love of playing in water. They will explore any body of water they come across, from a lake to a toilet.

GOOD DISCERNMENT

Teach me good discernment and knowledge,
For I believe in Your commandments.

Psalm 119:66 NASB

Water canals slice across the Italian plains. Our quaint village sometimes bore the side effects of these agricultural watering systems. The ditches became breeding grounds for rats that grew big and fat. They were a health hazard. Our exterminator was a black cat named Kimbo. He loved to deposit his trophies at our front door, but even Kimbo wasn't ready to tango with the monster in our garage.

My husband threw himself into the get-rid-of-the-rat mission. He cleaned, shifted storage boxes, and removed anything that might shelter the unwanted rodent. The garage sparkled.

My husband set traps, but the enormous rat carried them away. He bought bigger, more sophisticated traps. The rat managed to gnaw, wrestle, or heave itself free from every snare. Poison was the final option. My husband didn't want to unwittingly kill Kimbo or other animals. Admitting defeat, he planted some poison and put the rest of the box, full of poison packets, high on a shelf.

It must have been tasty, because after the rat ate the poison, he found the box and ate the rest of it.

We needed to find the corpse before Kimbo ate it. We looked everywhere, but Kimbo found it first. Fortunately, Kimbo recognized that the rat was poisoned. He scavenged it out but never bit into it. He knew a bad rat when he saw one.

The psalmist of Psalm 119:66 desired for God to teach him good discernment. The ability to judge between right and wrong is cultivated as we grow spiritually. In the Bible, the same Hebrew word for discernment sometimes refers to taste. We need the spiritual ability to perceive what is sweet, bitter, healthy, or poisonous to our souls. Discernment identifies what is wise or foolish, good or evil.

Later in Psalm 119, the author writes about God's Word tasting sweet like honey.

When we make a habit of ingesting God's truth, we learn how to separate truth from lies. Scripture offers great insight for wise living. Its words are sweet to our souls and bring understanding to our minds.

Dear Father, I know that your Word teaches me right from wrong. I want to make wise choices. Help me to discern what is good and what is evil, to understand what will help me and others become more like you. Keep me away from what might poison my mind and heart against you. Protect me from temptations that lead me astray. Thank you for the Bible through which you guide my life.

PAWS TO THINK

Are you facing some decisions
that need discernment? Where can you
find that discernment?

DID YOU KNOW

*Cats cannot taste sweet food,
and chocolate is poisonous to them.*

CAT DRAGGED IN

To obey is better than sacrifice,
and to listen than the fat of rams.

1 Samuel 15:22 esv

As Staci rounded the corner from the hallway to the living room, she stopped dead in her tracks. Callie, her adorable but devious calico cat, had done it again. Callie loved to hunt and bring home her prizes. This hunting trip had been very successful. In the middle of the hardwood floor was a collection of twigs, leaves, spiders, a worm, and one very large, furry mouse. A live mouse.

As a hunter, Callie was known for blessing her human family with a broad collection of gifts from the great outdoors. Although quite small, Callie moved with a grace and agility that outdid many other cats in the community. She moved quickly and purposefully when released from the house for her weekly excursions in the woods.

For the most part, her family could handle the woodsy gifts. It was the occasional animal (both dead and alive) that sent them over the edge. How did this cat manage to capture these large animals, and why did she think that her family needed them?

Callie was a bit of a kittycat packrat, content only when her hunting collection was at a premium. Dragging each new gift into the home merited more attention, and this packrat was all about increased attention.

I wonder how often we are guilty of the same approach with God. Are we potentially guilty of dragging our sacrificial gifts before God, for no other purpose than to get more attention? Are we trying to impress God for heavenly brownie points?

In the Old Testament, the Israelites often tried to please God with regular but mindless sacrifices, and that didn't go over very well. God is thrilled when we throw our energies into serving him. He prefers service over thoughtless sacrifice, just as he prefers a genuine heart over a self-absorbed spirit. Let's bring God only our purest intentions and service in the days ahead.

Father, in my rush to do the right thing, I sometimes cheapen your gift of grace by making a spectacle of my good deeds. You're not interested in a fancy show, nor will it give me a higher pedestal. You simply want my humble obedience. Give me the strength to make faith a natural part of my life, so I don't stand before you for superficial blessings. Never let me forget that my faith isn't about brownie points or star stickers. It is about investing in people for an eternal difference.

PAWS TO THINK

Do you make sacrifices to look good before God? How can you shift your focus to help others as God intended?

DID YOU KNOW

Cats have 1,000 times more data storage than an iPad.

HiGH AND MiGHTY

The LORD of hosts will have a day of reckoning
against everyone who is proud and lofty
and against everyone who is lifted up,
that he may be abased.

ISAIAH 2:12 NASB

Pumpkin, the orange and white tabby cat, was up to his old tricks. He stood at the sink, demanding water. While most cats are content with their daily water bowl, Pumpkin was unlike other cats and often displeased. At the ripe age of twenty, Pumpkin felt he'd earned the right to drink only the most purified and distilled water from the best sources. The common water bowl would no longer do. Saturday morning found His Majesty pacing at the kitchen sink, his sharp gaze saying, "Turn this faucet on before somebody gets hurt!"

Pumpkin was usually laid back, but his older cat years had thinned his patience and strengthened his persistence. Call it crankiness or entitlement, but Pumpkin had an attitude these days—a reality that left his owner perplexed.

What was it about filtered faucet water or bath-tub water that drew Pumpkin's interest? Why was some water randomly abandoned in favor of bottled water? Had Pumpkin turned into a health-conscious kitty cat? Perhaps his preferences were driven by changing taste buds or an altered state of self-importance.

We all have a little Pumpkin inside us. As hard as we try to remain humble, selfless, and low-maintenance, we are human. There are seasons when we believe we deserve only the best.

We need the best house, the most popular church, the latest fashions, the hippest restaurants, the flashiest car, and the most attractive spouse. After all, we work hard! We deserve to play hard and have the finest opportunities at our fingertips—right?

Wrong. God calls us to humility of thought and spirit, asking that we demand the finest only in our level of service to the kingdom. In his eyes, the finest is the purest worship, prayer, and intimacy with him. His finest requires our sincerest self before his throne. Humility carries more weight than haughtiness before the King.

Dear God, I want to crave the things that you crave. Help me exercise humility in everything, so I don't adopt a negative attitude that ruins my witness. Remind me that I should take the greatest pride in your presence and in your service. If I demand anything, let it be for more of you. Help me to daily set your wisdom and your ways higher than my own. Humble me in all things, that I may never mistake my own importance as highest priority.

PAWS TO THINK

How do you think your understanding of God would change if you took the greatest pride in knowing him more?

DID YOU KNOW

A cat ran for mayor of Mexico City in 2013.

HEAVEN'S GREATEST HOPE

Those who hope in the Lord will renew their strength.
They will soar on wings like eagles;
they will run and not grow weary,
they will walk and not be faint.

Isaiah 40:31 NIV

Where in the world is that cat?" Carol muttered to herself. She had spent the last half hour searching inside and out for her tabby cat, Hope. Hope had left home at least an hour ago and hadn't returned quickly, as she usually did. Carol needed to head to choir practice, but she was afraid to leave without knowing that Hope was safe and secure.

As time ticked by, Carol had an idea. The quiet evening filled with the first verse of "Joy to the World," and within moments, Hope bounded into the room.

Hope was a music-loving cat, mostly thanks to her musical owner. Carol loved to sing in community choirs. Music had always been a significant part of her life, especially during life's tragic and difficult seasons.

Music was there when Carol faced a difficult divorce

and went to the animal shelter to select a new cat—a cat she named Hope. Hope represented the advent of a new season of healing in Carol's life, a season of intimacy and trust with God.

As they bonded, Carol sang and whistled around Hope, choosing to whistle "Joy to the World" when calling her furry friend home. Hope was largely responsible for helping her owner rediscover joy in everyday living, so it was fitting that this song carried a special significance for cat and owner.

Believers should have the same response to our greatest hope and joy, Jesus Christ. Do we, like Hope, willingly return home to Jesus when he calls? Do we believe that he alone gives us the joy, peace, hope, and healing when we face life's darkest valleys?

Life is difficult, resulting in hurts and broken dreams that leave us despondent and downright hopeless. Sometimes, our first desire is to run far away from our feelings and into the arms of anything that can bring happiness.

God says, "Come to me. Only I can give what you desire. Let me hold and heal you. The world's joys are temporary." Let's make every effort to run toward our greatest joy and hope—Jesus.

Dear God, I rejoice in you as the creator and sustainer of all hope. Life is hard, and many things try to steal my joy. I often feel disheartened and discouraged, but you came to give us abundant life. Don't let me forget that this world cannot give me what you hold—eternal joy in a higher purpose. Remind me that you delight in who I am, and I can delight in the hope of Bethlehem and the healing of Calvary. I commit my discouraged feelings into your hands today. Thank you for the hope, healing, and joy you will foster in my heart.

PAWS TO THINK

Are their broken relationships in your life? How does it help to remember that God, who restores and brings hope to all things, is eager and willing to help you?

DID YOU KNOW

Cats rub and scratch as a form of communication.

GODLY GOOFBALL

He will yet fill your mouth with laughter,
and your lips with shouting.

JOB 8:21 ESV

Brenda heard the shredding paper and let out a heavy sigh. Dreamsicle, her three-month-old kitten, had destroyed an upper bookshelf last night. Books went flying as the kitten pushed herself onto the shelf for a better view of the family. This morning, destruction came as a ripped trash bag strewed garbage all over the kitchen floor. Now, the local newspaper was in a million little pieces, apparently to cushion Dreamsicle's afternoon nap. Dreamsicle was obviously quite comfortable in her new home.

Kittens are mischievous creatures, looking for their path in this big world. Their furry bodies create more than a few messes, but Dreamsicle took her kitten phase to the extreme. She would destroy anything in her path to reach a new destination, whether intentionally or unintentionally. She was an accident looking for a place to happen!

Her destructive habits were tempered by silliness.

Dreamsicle was a goofy little gal. She was capable of simultaneously destroying mom's decor while climbing into her lap for sweet cuddles. She would throw her tiny paw over her owner's heart, as if to say, "Remember that you love me."

In Dreamsicle's world, there was little acknowledgement of guilt. Instead, a sweet, humble spirit whispered, "Mommy, I didn't mean to make a mess. I love you." Little Dreamsicle regularly melted her owner's heart, even when covered in the debris of her latest escapade.

Some days, we're just like Dreamsicle. We don't try to create a mess—it just happens. At the end of the day, we shake off our mess and curl up in God's arms, whispering, "Father, I'm sorry. I didn't mean to hurt other people or disobey you. My emotions got the best of me today. I'm going to do better. I know you love me."

We all have a little goofiness that creates opportunities for accidental destruction. We're not perfect people. We regularly need repentance. We can place our hands over the master's heart, seeking his compassion. Whatever life tosses our way, we can stay close to his heart and hold his hand.

Father, I need you, sometimes more than I'm willing to admit. You are my hiding place even in the goofy parts of life. Thank you for catching me when I fall and loving me when I stray. Thank you for the gift of laughter and the permission to place my deepest thoughts and emotions at your feet even when they represent my most destructive intentions. Keep me close to you, so that even my silliness yields to greater service and my goofiness to deeper godliness. I love you and praise you.

PAWS TO THINK

Have you ever stopped to realize that your ability to laugh, play, run, and hide reflects the carefree and loving heart of your Savior?

DID YOU KNOW

Cats are the most popular pet in the UK and in the US.

PiNNED

Since we are surrounded by so great a cloud of witnesses,
let us also lay aside every weight, and sin which clings so closely,
and let us run with endurance the race that is set before us.

HEBREWS 12:1 ESV

"Ahhhh!" Tina's scream was one of the most bloodcurdling sounds ever heard. It woke the neighbors, rattled dishes, and shook curtains. Tina had reason to scream, because she entered the living room to find her cat, Murphy, quietly and calmly sitting on a long (and living!) snake. Murphy seemed rather pleased with himself. So pleased, in fact, that he continued smothering the snake and catching some morning sunbeams as mom ran out the door.

Murphy was persistent. In typical cat nature, Murphy loved to hunt and track down other creatures, but his expedition seemed to be about more than expanding his treasure trove. Many of Murphy's hunts looked less like typical cat nature and more like Murphy was making a point.

Some people claimed that Murphy was part human, as he possessed a level of persistence often associated with teenagers. Although sweet, Murphy could be stubborn and demanding when he wanted.

Murphy dragged that snake in for no other purpose than to sit on it. He didn't want to chase it, play with it, or even gift it. No, Murphy just wanted to sit on it, making a firm point about power and persistence. He could have sat there all day, had dad not removed his prize.

When I think about the power of sin in the life of the believer, I think about Murphy. Sin entraps and holds us down, stunting our growth with Jesus. Sin has the power and persistence to derail our faithfulness, and Satan is quite happy to let sin crush our heads and hearts so that we lose all belief in God.

When we are in a season of entrapment, we need to remember this; Satan has power, but he has no power over the Holy Spirit. Satan, like Murphy, might try to stop us, but we have victory over him through the blood of our King. We can escape sin's heavy hold by drawing closer to Calvary.

God, sin often entraps me. It robs me of my joy in you. I forget what it means to live a pure existence before your throne. The ways of this world are tempting, and they grab hold of my heart, promising great and wonderful treasures. In the end, they only disappoint. Help me repent and pursue holiness again. Remind me that you give me freedom over all that Satan brings my way. I surrender my desires and disobedience to you today, so nothing holds me down.

PAWS TO THINK

Have you ever wondered how God feels when we choose to stay trapped in sin instead of claiming freedom through our intimacy with him?

DID YOU KNOW

More cats are left-pawed than right.

PUBLICLY PERSISTENT

Do not grow weary in doing good.

2 THESSALONIANS 3:13 ESV

Precious was an athletic fur ball, driven by a love of ice hockey. Yes, you read that correctly. Precious loved nothing more than getting wild and crazy with slippery ice cubes on the tile floor. As her owner dropped cubes to the floor, she would bat the puck (ice cube) toward the net, which was a plastic shopping bag from the dollar store.

One Friday night, the game got a little too intense. Precious took the puck across the floor at breakneck speed, only to lose control, hit the trashcan, and tumble down the stairs into the laundry basket. The family suddenly had a cat who needed rescuing!

Mom and Dad were used to these athletic antics, but sometimes they landed Precious in hot water. Her ice hockey pursuits were no exception. Precious loved playing with her human father, rapidly moving the ice cube around the kitchen floor, playing keep-away or hide-and-seek among human legs.

The most admirable part of Precious' weekly adventures was her tenacity. No matter where the ice cube went or what obstacles got in her way, she kept at it, her body propelled by both momentum and persistence.

We could learn a thing or two from Precious, starting with her unabashed persistence before others. When I walk with the Lord, I want it to be a walk filled with the thrill and energy of cat ice hockey. I want to run, skip, speak, cry, sing, hope, and be who I am without shame before Christ. I want to feel complete freedom. Perhaps you do, too.

Sometimes, the weight of life's hardships and the fear of people's judgement shuts us down and restricts our freedom. We let fear replace faith and consequently lose our joy. That is not a happy place to be.

If that's where you are this week, run to God in prayer. Ask him to put the spiritual spark back into your heart so that you can run—like Precious—into his arms. Don't let Satan rob you of the excitement of living in the shadow of the Most Holy.

Father, I'm running to you today with my fear, worry, and stress. I want a faith that lets me be everything you designed me to be. Give me the joy and freedom to share honestly before your throne. When I grow weary, remind me that you call me to run my race with great delight. Help me run with abandon and embrace my call to share the Gospel story of your grace. Thank you for loving me in the crazy chaos of life and for helping me turn fear into an ever-growing faith.

PAWS TO THINK

How often do you take the time to come before God with childlike abandon and a spirited soul?

DID YOU KNOW

Over a short distance, a cat can travel at a top speed of thirty-one miles per hour.

SCENT OF THE SAVIOR

Whoever loves God is known by God.

1 CORINTHIANS 8:3 NIV

"If that cat escapes one more time, I'm going to lose my mind," Tigger's owner said, scowling. Tigger, a friendly calico cat, had escaped for the third time that year, and his owner was not pleased. As she repeatedly called his name and peered behind trash cans, parked cars, and tree stumps, Tigger took his sweet time strolling around the community.

After a long, frantic search, Tigger's mom was ready to give up and assume the worst. Tears in her eyes, she looked up and saw Tigger, sitting on their porch. Tigger was home.

Tigger made it home because he followed his scent. His owner knew that a cat's sense of direction is largely guided by smell, meaning a cat should recognize his or her own special scent. Mom had placed her four-legged son's shed fur around the front porch, in the flowerpots, and near the front steps. She wanted Tigger to know that this was home, where he was loved, fed, and protected.

Life gets so frenzied that we are often tempted to run for the door like Tigger. We grow weary of both mundane and stressful influences of this world, and we seek a quick escape into greener, more pleasurable pastures. After some time in those new pastures, the glam and glitter wear off. Fun fades into oblivion, leaving us in the same spot as before. We realize that it's time to return to family and friends—and to our Father, who is always whispering, "Come home to me."

Fortunately, Scripture reminds us that, like Tigger, we know the way home. We can pick up the scent of God's presence and power in his Word. The Bible is our best map, leading us back to the fold of the One who promises to never forsake us.

Whenever we feel lost, we need to grab a Bible and begin the journey home to our Father. We get quiet before him, seek wisdom in his words, and absorb his fail-proof direction. His way will lead to perfect peace.

Father, your patience amazes me. You tolerate my pursuits for greener pastures that rarely lead to anything positive or productive. I want to stay close to you—to hear you speak, feel your comfort, and rest in your peace, but I tend to wander. Please challenge me to pick up my Bible roadmap every day. Let me explore the wonder of your wisdom, ask questions, and meditate on your faithfulness. Protect me from all that threatens to steal my time with you.

PAWS TO THINK

Is God saddened when you are lost and struggling to find your way back to him? Where do you see that in the Bible?

DID YOU KNOW

Cats have a highly developed sense of smell, composed of over nineteen million receptors.

TRUST HIS TIMING

My times are in your hands;
deliver me from the hands of my enemies,
from those who pursue me.

PSALM 31:15 NIV

If there was one thing that little Petunia didn't need for Christmas, it was a watch. Petunia always knew what time it was. The shorthaired kitty was Type-A all the way. Every morning, she followed the same routine. Long before any alarm clock, Petunia climbed onto her owner's bed, took her little paw, and tapped his forehead insistently.

Unfortunately for Pete, the owner, a bitterly cold, snowy morning was no exception to the rule. Despite his desire to hibernate as the snow fell, Petunia was adamant about keeping to the daily schedule. At 4:30, the tapping ritual began.

For a while, Pete tried to play dead, but this approach did nothing to deter Petunia. She wanted her owner up without delay. Next, Pete built a bigger fort of blankets around his body, using pillows as lookout points. This tactic proved useless. Petunia kept checking her internal kitty clock, and she knew time was wasting away. There were too many things to get done today. She kept tapping Pete's forehead until his feet finally hit the floor.

When I think about Pete and his precocious Petunia, I can't help but chuckle. Pet owners understand the struggle of wanting to stay in bed, despite a pet's persistence. I also admire Petunia, because she recognized the seriousness of scheduled time.

In our walk with Jesus, we can sometimes lose sight of the schedule. God's Word tells us how to fill our time. We should be busy sharing the Gospel, meeting needs, and ministering to hurting souls—the highest priorities over anything else on our to-do list.

We can always trust God's perfect timing for our lives. We can keep a schedule of service before the throne. We need to embrace Petunia's persistence in matters of faith and the pursuit of people who need God's love and compassion. We can work on God's schedule until he returns.

Father, I recognize that my time is your time. My timing is rarely your timing, and that's okay. Remind me of the purpose you gave me, the call to fill my days and nights with more of you. I want to wake up energized each day, fulfilling my higher, heavenly purpose instead of hibernating under the weight of this world's worries. Keep me diligent in my Christian walk and help me set a schedule that brings the story of your grace to others.

PAWS TO THINK

Where can you schedule time
to serve God?

DID YOU KNOW

The most popular pedigree cat is the Persian cat, followed by the Maine coon cat and the Siamese cat.

FANCY AND FORMAL

"You must be careful to do everything they tell you. But do not do what they do, for they do not practice what they preach."

MATTHEW 23:3 NIV

The house was in total disarray. The laundry needed folding. The counter was a mess. Fallen leaves needed to be raked, bagged, and discarded. There was too much to do, and mom was at her breaking point. When all hope seemed lost, Mr. Fritzy entered the scene. Mom first saw the black paws, followed by the white stripe, and finally the freckled face.

Mr. Fritzy, whose fur resembled a tuxedo, climbed up on the counter, sat down elegantly, and looked deep into his owner's weary eyes. "Are you ready to hit the town?" his gaze said. "It's party time!"

Mr. Fritzy was a fun, fancy, formal-loving cat who carried himself above the rest of the kitty kingdom. Inside that natural furry tuxedo was an attitude that rivaled any teenager's. In Fritzy's mind, he was "all that and a bag of chips." He couldn't be bothered with the messy or mundane. He lived high-class, prancing around the house with step that screamed, "I'm better than you!"

In Fritzy's mind, he was king of the jungle. He wanted people to come when he called and play when he said play. He wasn't interested in lowering his self-appointed first-class status to help anyone.

In many ways, Fritzy reminds us of the Pharisees in the New Testament. They were self-absorbed hypocrites who thought they could tell believers what, how, and when they should worship God. They weren't willing to dirty their hands or follow Christ in serving the vulnerable.

Like Fritzy, we're all guilty of putting on our formal tuxedos at times. We strut into the community, motivated by a deep need for others to notice our glimmering halos. Jesus tells us to remain humble and holy, giving up the fancy and formal for the simple pleasures of faith.

When we lose sight of the honor of being with our King, we need to lay aside our massive to-do lists, take off our formal attire, and curl up in our pajamas to talk to him. He yearns to hear our voices.

Father, I need humility. I'm so self-absorbed at times that I fail to live in the purity and passion of faithful service. Help me to avoid turning into a fancy, formal hypocrite who is only concerned with what people think. Instead, make me kind, genuine, and sincere, driven by the things that touch your heart. Whenever I'm tempted to place myself above my brothers and sisters in Christ, stop me. I should only reflect your Holy Spirit. Strengthen my yearning for deeper humility as I grow in your holiness.

PAWS TO THINK

How can you avoid becoming
self-absorbed and motivated
only by what others think?

DID YOU KNOW

*Cats spend about a third of the day grooming.
the backwards-facing spikes on their tongues
speed up the process. That's why their tongues
feel rough, like sandpaper.*

VANISHING VISITOR

"Behold, I stand at the door and knock.
If anyone hears my voice and opens the door,
I will come in to him and eat with him, and he with me."

REVELATION 3:20 ESV

The tapping on the window increased. Cynthia walked to the cupboard, poured out some cat food, and fluffed up her comforter. Within minutes, Rama the cat entered her apartment via the deck door. He gobbled up the cat food, fluffed his tail, and passed out in the middle of her bed, drifting off for a peaceful afternoon nap. There was one little problem with this afternoon siesta—this wasn't Rama's home.

You might be tempted to label Rama an interloper, but he was warmly welcomed. In fact, everyone in this New York neighborhood loved the affable neighborhood cat. Although well cared for by his family, Rama was a wanderer.

Rama would eagerly eat your food, take a respite on your freshly washed sheets, and drop a few cat hairs on the floor before heading home. His visits were short and sweet—a quick hello before disappearing over the window ledge.

When I think about Rama's rather self-centered visits, I wonder if we do the same to God. Are we guilty of coming to him only when we need something? Perhaps we come into God's presence just long enough to grab a snack, find relief from life's storms, and ask for thirty-second answers to our deepest prayers. We enter his presence in desperation, but we aren't willing to stay long. We're in and out of his heavenly home without even hanging our coats in the closet.

Temporary visits with God are like visiting a vending machine. We turn to one when we want something, like a tasty candy bar, but we quickly move on to the next desire once the candy is in hand. That approach doesn't work with God. He's eternal, not temporary. He wants long-term visits where we wrestle with biblical principles and promises and absorb his greatest wisdom.

If we're guilty of short visits with God, we need to pray for the desire to stay longer. We're never interlopers before our Savior. His door is always open.

Father, thank you for opening the door and welcoming me home. Help me to desire nothing more than stillness in your presence. You're not interested in vending machine visits—you want to spend quality time by my side. Thank you for not giving up on me when I take advantage of your goodwill. I want to grow in my faith and learn to desire hours of conversation every day. Slow me down, so that I learn to value humility and holiness.

PAWS TO THINK

How can you pursue
longer visits with God?

DID YOU KNOW

From two weeks of age, cats need to interact with people to successfully socialize with humans later in life.

IT'S DARK IN HERE!

You will light my lamp;
The Lord my God will enlighten my darkness.

Psalm 18:28 NKJV

Recently, a stray cat living at a local fire station made the news with his disappearance. The firefighters looked everywhere for Flame, their "arson cat." They called for him and checked the parking lot. As one firefighter walked the back perimeter of the property, he heard a noise from the storm drain. It was not your usual meowing or purring, but a desperate cry filled with fear. Flame was trapped in the drainpipe.

Flame continued to cry until firefighters rescued him. They never found out how he got into the drain or how long he'd been crying out, hoping someone would find him.

Very few of us know what it is like to be stuck in a storm drain. We can only imagine the loneliness and darkness. However, most of us know what it's like to be in a situation where we feel hopeless, alone, and trapped in darkness.

We don't know how we are going to get out. We can't find a way. We desperately seek the One who is the light.

Like Flame, we cry for help. We want nothing more than to escape the darkness and walk into the light. At first, we cry out softly, but soon we're pleading for a solution to our circumstances.

God is called light in numerous places in the Bible. He is a lamp for our feet, and a light for our paths, and he will bring light to what is hidden in darkness. We have constant access to his light through prayer, the Word, and the counsel of others.

When we put our trust in God, we have assurance that, no matter how dark life seems, we only have to reach out for the light. That light is extra welcome when you've been in the dark.

Father, some of my circumstances are pretty dark right now. I live in a world full of suffering and pain. I know the answer to the darkness that surrounds me—you. You are the light of the world. No matter how dark it gets, I can count on you to illuminate the dark places. I cry out to you! Come into my life. Fill me with your light. When your light is within me, I am never truly in the dark.

PAWS TO THINK

Think about the dark places in your life. What can you do to let the light of Jesus fill them?

DID YOU KNOW

Cats have up to a hundred different vocalizations.

WORTH CHASING

Choose my instruction instead of silver,
knowledge rather than choice gold.

PROVERBS 8:10 NIV

When Country had a litter of kittens, her family kept one and named her Callie. Country went in and out, but Callie stayed in the basement. Then, Country began carrying live chipmunks into the house and turning them loose. It wasn't her normal behavior, and everyone was puzzled.

Country wasn't bringing chipmunks to her human family. She brought them to Callie. Since Callie wasn't going outdoors, Country found a creative way to teach her how to hunt. Country was preparing Callie to live outdoors and become a grown-up cat.

Fortunately, parents don't have to teach children how to catch live chipmunks running through the house. Feline or human, parents do have a responsibility to teach their children. What are the best ways to teach children the life lessons they need to survive?

Teach by example. Country brought the chipmunk

to Callie so she could show her the technique. We can model love and kindness when we interact with others. The greatest lessons often come from observation, not communication.

Teach by soft instruction. Loud instruction is almost always yelling in a child's mind even though our volume may not change much. We should keep our voices at a soothing level and our demeanors calm.

Teach by positive expectation. We should expect the best from our children, but all children make mistakes. All children need guidance. All are made in the image of God. If we make a mistake, we should continue our modeling by admitting we were wrong and apologizing.

Teach with love. No matter what the lesson, our love for our children should be the strongest emotion they receive.

As God's child, you may find yourself on the other end of instruction. We must be open to his teaching and guidance. His wisdom is there for us when we study his Word and spend time listening for his voice.

God wants us to feel loved and prepared for the "hunts" in our lives. He doesn't want us chasing the wrong things.

Father, I know you love me and want me to grow into your plans for me. Sometimes the lessons are hard. Help me open up to your teaching. When I am a slow learner, gently remind me of your love. When I struggle to succeed, encourage me and show me how to accomplish my goals. When I learn to follow you in areas of life, celebrate with me and draw me closer. I long to be a good student. I want to make you proud.

PAWS TO THINK

What was the most recent lesson God taught you? Were you a good student, or should you ask him to help you grow more in that area?

DID YOU KNOW

A group of kittens is called a kindle.

PERSEVERE

You need to persevere so that when you have done the will of God,
you will receive what he has promised.

HEBREWS 10:36 NIV

While Daniel was mowing his yard, he discovered a feral cat nursing her kittens. His family provided food for the newly named Bran (short for Bran Muffin) and kept watch as Bran moved her brood from place to place to protect them. Once the kittens were old enough to be adopted, Daniel's family took the kittens to the shelter so they could join loving families.

The plan was to leave Mama Bran there as well. However, since she'd never been petted and would likely be euthanized, the family had Bran spayed and took her back home. It was three years before Bran finally let someone touch her. Still skittish, she often shows her gratitude for the family's kindness by leaving trophies of her hunting expeditions at the back steps.

Many situations require perseverance. Perseverance is a big word, but accomplishing it requires tiny steps. Bran's family didn't bring her home and pet her and smother her with love. They continued to talk to her, feed her, meet her basics needs, and make her feel welcome. After years of kindness, Bran was ready to move closer and let them gently pet her.

The reward for perseverance is sometimes immediate. We will probably succeed at threading a needle if we keep trying. Success comes in steps as we cook and produce a fancy dinner. Successful dieting can take months to show results. If we are redirecting a habit, the change may take years.

To grow spiritually, we must spend time with God. Distractions in our daily lives tend to thwart our efforts. The enemy likes to see that happen. We need to stand firm. Even if our day is filled with distractions, we need to spend time with God before bed. We must press on and put our relationship with God first. That is the ultimate perseverance—a lifelong goal to draw closer to our Creator.

Perseverance takes planning. Let's set our goals and focus on the things we want to accomplish for God.

Father, thank you for being patient when I don't learn lessons the first time. Give me strength and endurance to keep trying to meet my goals. My highest goal is to please you in everything I do. Sometimes I do a good job; other times I fall short. Celebrate the victories with me and give me peace when success takes a lot of work. You are in charge of my goals, and I can rest confidently in your plans. Thank you for that assurance.

PAWS TO THINK

What goal took you years to accomplish? How did you feel when you achieved success?

DID YOU KNOW

Some 700 million feral cats live in the United States. Many shelters run trap-neuter-release programs to stem population growth.

PURPOSE

We know that in all things God works for the good of those who
love him, who have been called according to his purpose.

ROMANS 8:28 NIV

Dalene watched as an older gentleman entered the vet's office with a colorful cat carrier. She complimented it, and they struck up a conversation. She learned he and his wife cared for several dozen animals at their home. The couple had figured out how to identify each cat and pair it with the correct carrier, and they considered every one part of their large family.

"Our daughter and her family live in Florida, so we don't get to see them much," Mr. Yancy said. "My wife and I decided to rescue animals. These cats give us purpose since no family is around." He smiled. "It's a lot of work with so many, but you do what it takes."

Without a purpose, we struggle to find validation and worth. How can we find our life's purpose? Many people advise looking at our passions. Others ask what energizes us. Purpose is more than this. Purpose is the discovery of the people God created us to be. In the movie *Chariots of Fire*, we see Eric Liddell struggle to find his life's purpose. He tries to articulate this to his sister by saying, "When I run, I feel God's pleasure."

Most of us wonder from time to time about our purpose in life. When we understand that God loves us and created us for his purpose, our struggle lessens. We were created for certain tasks, and we understand that everything works together to accomplish God's plan for our lives. When we are confused about our purpose, we should spend extra time in God's Word and talk to him more. We must be still, listening for his instruction as he leads us from one season to another.

Mr. Yancy and his wife found purpose by caring for their cat family in the absence of their children. Fulfilling God's purpose in our lives is a privilege. We intertwine our lives with God's purpose to reach others with his message of hope.

Father, it is so good to know that I have a purpose in this world, and that purpose is part of your master plan! Don't let me get caught up in wondering what my purpose is. Keep my eyes on you. Reveal to me my tasks for this season in my life. Assure me that, whatever that is, you will equip me for the task. I love being part of your plan. Thank you for creating me with specific skills and dreams.

PAWS TO THINK

Do you know what your purpose is for this season? When do you feel God's pleasure?

DID YOU KNOW

Owning a cat can reduce the risk of stroke and heart attack by a third.

SPECIFIC PRAYER

"If you believe, you will receive whatever you ask for in prayer."

MATTHEW 21:22 NIV

Five-year-old Chris was understandably heartbroken when his kitten was accidentally hit and killed by a car. "We will pray that God sends another kitty," his mom and dad said. Every night, Chris prayed for a new kitten, specifically God to send a black and white one. He asked his brothers and sisters to pray, too, so they joined him.

A few weeks later, a neighbor phoned. "There's a stray kitten hanging around our house, and we can't keep it. Our dogs would not be happy. Would you like to have it?" When the neighbor visited, a black and white kitten meowed from his arms.

"God heard my prayers!" Chris said. Fred quickly became a family favorite.

Often, we pray generic prayers, like "God bless the world," or "Lord, help my family." Those are good prayers, but as relationship with God grows, we become more specific and honest in our conversations, just as we do with friends.

Think about family relationships. We know many relatives well. When our siblings or grown children visit, we don't say, "How are the things in your world?" We want to know specifics. "How is the new neighborhood?" "Are you still undecided about the new school for the children?" "Are you getting along better with your boss?"

Specific prayers exhibit our trust in God. He knows our hearts, but when we verbalize desires to him in specific words, we show him that we understand he answers our prayers and provides for our needs.

Chris could have prayed, "God, please send me a new pet." He asked for a kitten—a black and white kitten. God heard his prayer and answered it.

Father, I want to trust you with the desires of my heart. I fear that if I pray too specifically, I could be disappointed. Grow my trust in you. You are not the God of disappointment but the God of provision. If I ask you for something, you don't deny me because you don't love me. You have a better way to answer my prayer. You want what is best for me, and I don't want to forget that. May I pray confidently and specifically.

PAWS TO THINK

What are the things you are praying for right now? Are you praying specifically?

DID YOU KNOW

There are cats who have survived falls from over 32 stories onto concrete.

FISH OR KITTEN?

"You did not choose me, but I chose you and appointed you so that you might go and bear fruit—fruit that will last—and so that whatever you ask in my name the Father will give you."

JOHN 15:16 NIV

Susanne bounced into the pet shop. She had been begging for a pet for a long time, and her mom had finally agreed to a goldfish. Susanne went through the door and headed straight for the fish. As she walked down the first aisle, however, she stopped. There were crates full of kittens. Susanne stopped at one in the middle. There, a little black kitten was literally climbing the walls trying to get out. She calmed down as Susanne stroked her.

"Mom?" Susanne's yearning face asked the rest of the question.

"Susanne, we came to get a fish, not a kitten. A kitten needs a lot more care than a fish."

"But this one needs a home! The fish don't care as long as they have water. I want this kitten instead of a fish. Please?" Susanne pleaded. "I'll take good care of it."

Choices, choices. We make thousands every day, beginning with getting out of bed, deciding what to wear, making cereal or eggs for breakfast...the list goes on and on. Many are harder than choosing between a fish and a kitten.

Some choices are fun choices. Some are easy, others hard and life-changing. Tough choices have the potential to chart the course of our lives. Who to marry, where to go to college, and when to buy a house. When faced with the challenging choices and situations, do we choose to be overcomers or victims? Do we respond to God's offer of eternal life through Jesus, or do we choose a hopeless life without him?

God has already chosen us to be his children. He offers his love to everyone. We don't have to work to receive his love; he gives it regardless of our choices.

Every day is a clean slate. The choices we made yesterday are gone. We can choose to make today a better day by being diligent and serving God. Why not make that our first choice every morning?

Father, I want to make good choices. You can help me do that. I ask for your guidance. I want to follow you and I want to do a good job of it. I want people to see the way I live and the decisions I make and see that I depend on you. Speak to those who have refused your love. Let them know that you have already chosen them.

PAWS TO THINK

What is the hardest choice you made today? Was it a good one?

DID YOU KNOW

Only 11.5% of people consider themselves cat people.

CONSTANT COMFORT

Praise be to the God and Father of our Lord Jesus Christ,
the Father of compassion and the God of all comfort,
who comforts us in all our troubles,
so that we can comfort those in any trouble
with the comfort we ourselves receive from God.

2 CORINTHIANS 1:3-4 NIV

Amy Rose and her family adopted Tippy to keep their other cat company. She tipped her head slightly when she listened to voices. Tippy was uniquely adorable—black with tips of white on her ears, nose, and tail.

Tippy started to feel unwell. After a trip to the vet and a round of antibiotics, she was no better. On her return appointment, the vet discovered that Tippy was suffering from cancer in multiple parts of her body.

"Mom, she was only a year old," Amy Rose sobbed over the phone. "This hurts so bad."

"Saying good-bye hurts," her mother said sadly. "But we continue to adopt pets because the unconditional relationships we have with our animals is life-giving—for them and for us."

Pets like Tippy quickly become part of our families. We love them, and they return our love. We build relationships with them as we do other family members. They become our fast friends, encouragers, comforters, listeners, and more. When they die, we grieve their loss.

It's hard to come to terms with loss, particularly when the loss seems premature. It helps to concentrate on all the good memories. Even though Tippy only lived with Amy Rose and her family for a year, she gave a year of loving memories. The family can look at pictures and talk about the good times.

We can turn saying good-bye to a pet into a positive experience. We can look for another kitten to rescue, or perhaps an older cat needs a good home. We have so much love to give.

When we deal with grief over our cats, we must remember that God understands. Our kittens were his creations. He knows our heartache and pain, and he will be our comfort.

Father, thank you for your constant comfort in every situation. You understand that losing a pet is painful. It's hard to have someone or something taken away. Thankfully, your love can never be taken away. Today I pray for those hurting from the pain of losing a loved one, and also for people who don't understand how your constant comfort could touch their lives. Speak to them today and draw them close to you.

PAWS TO THINK

What was the greatest comfort to you during a time of loss? How can you reach out to others who have recently lost?

DID YOU KNOW

When a family cat died in ancient Egypt, family members shaved off their eyebrows in mourning.

WATCHING OR SERVING?

Do not be slothful in zeal, be fervent in spirit, serve the Lord.

ROMANS 12:11 ESV

Denise and Rick sat in the den, watching television. Shadow was sleeping between them. All was calm until Denise saw movement in the corner of the room. A tiny mouse scampered across the floor.

"C'mon, Shadow," Rick said as he and Denise got up to begin the mouse hunt. Shadow stretched and rolled over, oblivious to the urgency of the situation. Denise and Rick chased the mouse into the dining room and cornered it behind a tall floor speaker.

"I'm going to lie on the floor on this side so he can't escape. You shoo it over here," Rick said to Denise. As Denise closed in, the little mouse leaped over Rick and escaped out the patio door.

During the entire twenty-minute episode, Shadow watched the entertainment.

Each of us has had occasions where we acted like

Shadow. We kept our distance, observed what was going on, and never offered to assist, though we were qualified to do the job.

Unfortunately, this also happens in the church. We hear announcements that they need more nursery workers or Vacation Bible School volunteers. Perhaps it's a plea to visit people in the community.

Deep down, we want to help, but we often think that plenty of people will volunteer. We'll just wait until next time. We sit back and watch others serve. No one wants to be called a sloth, but if we only observe opportunities, we haven't succeeded in doing our jobs. We are being lazy.

You may not be the best at answering the call for big group events. Perhaps your gift is one-on-one relationships. You could mentor neighbors or younger ladies, take senior citizens grocery shopping, or babysit for a single mom to give her a night out. All of these are important service to God. Don't be a Shadow! Use your talents to serve.

Father, I don't want to be a sloth. Show me new ways I can serve you. I know there are many places in my church, community, and family where I can step up and encourage others. I want to be known as someone who does your business, always willing to help someone else. You made us to serve others as your hands and feet. Help me fulfill that purpose.

PAWS TO THINK

Make a list of your talents and interests. How could you use them to serve others?

DID YOU KNOW

Cats sleep for 70% of their lives.

ASK BOLDLY

Let us then approach God's throne of grace with confidence,
so that we may receive mercy and find grace to help us
in our time of need.

HEBREWS 4:16 NIV

Our cat is a precious princess. Emily knows that she is loved, and it never occurs to her that she might not be the center of our universe. It wasn't always that way. We had two dogs when we brought Emily home as a tiny kitten. She was unsure about the furry beasts, but it didn't take long before she said her piece and they left her alone.

It was a peaceful existence, and we assumed everyone was satisfied with the arrangement. However, fast-forward ten years, and Emily is the only pet we have. We've noticed a remarkable change in her attitude since our dogs passed away. Instead of being droopy, she's blossomed into a truly happy cat. In the shadow of our dogs, she tended to be shy and quiet. Now she prances through the house like she owns it—in fact, she probably does.

She no longer has to compete for lap space or skulk

around, waiting for us to notice her. We assumed that behavior had been normal cat reticence. But now, when she wants our attention, she boldly claims time in our arms. Sometimes she stalks the house, calling out confidently to let us know she wants to spend time with us. Every time she asks for my attention, it warms my heart.

It's easy to skulk around the edges of God's presence, hoping he'll notice us. It can seem like there is too much competition, and that there are too many others with greater need for his attention. That couldn't be further from the truth.

God wants us to have Emily's confidence in our time with him. We're his precious children, and he wants us to approach him knowing we're loved and wanted. It thrills his heart when we ask for his attention and insist on time alone with him.

Dear Lord, don't let me hesitate about approaching you. You tell me that I'm your precious child, yet I don't act like I believe it. I worry about bothering you with little things. You care about me, and you care about the things that are important to me. Help me to come boldly for your attention. Keep me from tiptoeing around the edges, so I won't miss spending precious time with you.

PAWS TO THINK

Have you been hesitant about approaching God? What are you going to do about it?

DID YOU KNOW

Domesticated cats use vocalizations like meowing, purring, and hissing—but feral cats are practically silent.

HERE KITTY!

The LORD is my light and my salvation; whom shall I fear?
The LORD is the stronghold of my life; of whom shall I be afraid?

PSALM 27:1 ESV

One-year-old Bella went outside one afternoon. The yellow tiger cat loved to go out and roam around, but she always came back by dark. That day, she didn't come home. Pat and Jane called and called her name, with no response.

Almost thirty-six hours later, Bella reappeared. They couldn't imagine where she'd been or what she had done. After that episode, Bella refused to go outside. She didn't go outside for two years.

They never figured out exactly what happened to Bella, but friends with a similar experience suggested that Bella was most likely treed. She probably spent those thirty-six hours trying to find a way to come down without detection from whatever had scared her up into the tree. Paralyzed by fear, she wouldn't have moved until she felt safe enough.

Have you ever felt paralyzing fear? Most of us have had

mental "treeings" in our lives. Instead of being in a tree, we sat on the fence. Maybe you couldn't decide which choice was best for your family. Perhaps a relationship needed mending, and you didn't know where to start.

Psalm 27:1 reminds us that no fear can truly paralyze us. As believers, we have the assurance of salvation and the promise of God's constant presence. If we are caught in a physical problem, God's strength can become ours. If there are decisions to be made, God's wisdom can guide us. If we need to mend a relationship, God has already prepared the way.

Next time we feel paralyzed or afraid, we can let God be our stronghold and our strength. We can call out to him.

Father, you know how terrified I can be. Sometimes, the situation warrants that kind of fear. Other times, I have let fear grow out of proportion. You are always there to calm my fears. Keep my mind and thoughts focused on you so I will naturally speak your name in the middle of my fears. Thank you for your presence and for reminding me that you're with me. Keep me focused on you.

PAWS TO THINK

Think of a time when you were paralyzed by fear. What did you learn about your relationship with God during that time?

DID YOU KNOW

Cats have inferior daytime sight, but during the night they need seven times less light than humans to see.

IMPROVED HEALTH

I pray that all may go well with you and that you may be
in good health, as it goes well with your soul.

3 John 1:2 ESV

Patrick worked at a local golf course. One afternoon, he
saw several cart boys gathered around something on the
ground. He walked over and discovered a scrawny yellow
kitten lapping from a saucer. "Look, Mr. Patrick, we found
a kitten!" one of them said. "We're trying to keep her fed.
We know she likes milk, but we gave her cream instead so
she could grow faster."

"I'm glad you're taking care of her," Patrick said, "But
cream isn't good for kittens. Why don't we try to find her a
home and get her food that's made for kittens?"

Patrick took the kitten home with him. He and his wife
nursed the kitty back to health. Tigress is now a member
of the family and travels everywhere with them in their
motorhome.

Like the cart boys, have you ever thought that richer,
creamier, and sweeter things are better for you than basic,

natural foods? Our country has an epidemic of such thinking. The Bible tells us that good health "goes well with your soul." When we take care of God's temple, we're improving our spiritual health. Many people don't consider that connection, but it's vital to our overall wellbeing.

Imagine if someone asked you about your spiritual health. "Would you do anything you could to grow spiritually and become closer to God?" Most of us wouldn't hesitate to reply in the affirmative. What if they rephrased the question: "Do you know that good physical health is important to a healthy spiritual life?" Many of us would look at them in shock.

We need to take stock of what we're feeding our temple, physically and spiritually. To operate at optimum levels, we need the good stuff. God has all the spiritual food we need in his Word. Let's get a good dose of physical and spiritual nutrition every day.

Father, thank you for making me your temple. I know you designed my physical health and my spiritual health to work together, but sometimes I give in to things that aren't good for me. Fill me with the desire to keep your temple clean and holy, so I can best serve you. I need to be healthy to do your work. I place my physical and spiritual health in your hands. Strengthen me and make me an effective servant of your kingdom.

PAWS TO THINK

What can you do to improve your physical and spiritual health?

DID YOU KNOW

Cats are often lactose intolerant, so milk isn't always best for them.

A GOOD NAME

A good name is to be chosen rather than great riches,
and favor is better than silver or gold.

PROVERBS 22:1 ESV

During a piano lesson in Arkansas, Chelsea Clinton saw a cat outside the window. She rescued the shorthair tuxedo cat and named him Socks for the markings on his feet. When the family moved to the White House, Socks quickly assumed the role of Chief Executive Cat.

While in the White House, Socks received fan mail and became a celebrity. Hilary Clinton took him to visit senior citizens and children. He appeared with President Clinton on a series of stamps in the Central African Republic. Cat lovers mourned his passing at the age of twenty.

Socks received his name because it was descriptive. He received his legacy because of who he was and what he did.

In the Bible, James and John were called the Sons of Thunder. Jesus called Peter the Rock. People often refer to David as a man after God's own heart. Athletes receive nicknames because of their appearance or their stellar performances.

How did you get your name? Is it descriptive? Was it passed down as a gift from a family member?

While some people are given labels based on looks, the most important name comes from what is inside. A good name doesn't come from what you look like. It comes from the godly characteristics that you possess. People who have a good name are kind, trustworthy, humble, noble, and honest. Those with a good name exhibit the love of Christ in everything they do.

What words do people use to describe you? Would they look at your outward appearance, or would their first impressions reflect your Christ-like qualities?

Father, I want to be just like you. I want to love others in a way that shows inner goodness. Even though I'm not perfect, I know you forgive me whenever I fail. Help me to exhibit the qualities of Jesus in everything I do. When people look at me, I want them to see kindness, thoughtfulness, trustworthiness, honesty, and the like. Show me ways to serve others.

PAWS TO THINK

Have you thought about your name lately? What would you like your spiritual name to reflect?

DID YOU KNOW

Cats have a unique vocabulary with their owners. Each cat has a different set of vocalizations, purrs, and behaviors.

THE ANGEL CAT

He will command his angels concerning you
to guard you in all your ways.

PSALM 91:11 ESV

Chuck sat alone on the front porch feeling lost. Just a week ago, he and his wife had spent hours here, talking and enjoying a spring afternoon. Now she was gone, and Chuck didn't have anyone to talk to. As lonely thoughts ran through his head, Chuck felt something brush up against his leg. He looked down to see a cat with black and white fur. She circled his legs and began to explore the rest of the porch.

Once the cat decided this was a good place to rest, she curled up on a pillow Chuck had laid beside his chair. She appeared relaxed and happy to have found a spot to rest. "So, you were lonely, too," Chuck said. "What's your name? I'm going to call you Ghost. You knew I could use a friend today." The cat's eyes watched Chuck as he spoke, then they closed. "Sleep well," Chuck said, smiling. "I'm going to give it a shot myself."

Ghost helped Chuck through his loneliest days after his wife's death. They sat on the porch together every day. After several months, Ghost disappeared, and Chuck never saw her again. From that point on, he called Ghost "the angel cat."

Angels appear during times of need, helping us through the valleys of life. If we could view the spiritual realm, we would see the many times God has sent an angel to help us.

Have you ever seen an angel? Maybe it was in the form of a friend. For Chuck, it was in the form of a cat named Ghost.

Father, you are always with me and your angels are around me. Thank you for the times I have known they were there, as well as the times I didn't realize they were working hard on my behalf. Maybe you can use me as a human angel. I am willing, and I want to work for your kingdom in any way I can. What a privilege to be used that way! It is a comfort to know that I can count on your protection. Your angels are constantly at work.

PAWS TO THINK

Can you remember a time when you were aware of God's angel in your life?

DID YOU KNOW

Cats mark you as their territory when they rub against you. They have scent glands in their faces and bodies.

JOY IN HARDSHIP

Consider it all joy, my brethren,
when you encounter various trials.

JAMES 1:2 NASB

Emily had been our cat for twelve years when she got sick. She started losing weight and drinking lots of water. We took her to the vet and learned she had hyperthyroidism. This diagnosis meant she'd be on medicine for the rest of her life.

At first, I was so relieved her condition was treatable that I didn't realize how difficult it was going to be to give a cat a pill—twice a day. Her tiny mouth made it almost impossible for me to poke the pill down her throat, and she was too smart to eat something with the pill hidden inside.

We went back to the vet for a solution. He explained that cats were motivated by food. If we sandwiched the pill popping in between treats, she'd be much happier about the situation. He also provided a plastic syringe that held the pill, making it possible to place the medicine at the back of her mouth so that she had to swallow it.

Within a few days, we had a routine. We'd place two small treats in her favorite perch. She'd leap up, eat the treats, and then we'd administer the pill, following up with two more treats. One day, we were in a hurry and forgot our routine. Emily set up a yowling that could have awakened the dead. She wanted her treats, and she wanted them right now!

I rushed to do her feline bidding and couldn't help but grin. She'd taken a bad situation and flipped it upside down, turning it into something that brought her joy.

God provides opportunities for joy no matter the stress or struggle we face. We always have a choice to focus on the struggle or the good that comes out of it. God wants us to face our difficulties like Emily. He wants us to find the joy and use it to lift our spirits.

Dear Lord, I long to look at life like Emily did. She took something that should have made her miserable and turned it into something she looked forward to. Show me how to find the positive in the difficult situations. Remind me that there are always reasons to be joyful. You have poured out countless blessings on me and on those I love, yet I still look for the smallest speck of hardship. Work in my heart and change my attitude from the inside out.

PAWS TO THINK

How can you look at a current situation differently and find joy in it?

DID YOU KNOW

There are an estimated 200-600 million cats alive on earth.

WARMED BY THE LIGHT

"The light shines in the darkness,
and the darkness can never extinguish it."

JOHN 1:5 NLT

My cat is my constant companion. She prefers to be in my lap or within petting distance. When I'm working in my home office, that's not possible. I've never found an efficient way to work on the computer and pet her, so she's content napping nearby while I work.

I was cleaning my office and realized that she didn't have a single favorite spot in that room. Instead, there were half a dozen areas covered with cat fur. That seemed odd. In our family room, she has one favorite place in front of the big window.

I began watching her behavior when I brought my coffee upstairs and began work. She settled into a spot on the floor near the door. When I came back up after lunch, she'd moved to the squishy red ottoman with cozy afghan. Later in the afternoon, I noticed her curled in the overstuffed chair in the corner.

After typing the last word for the day, she was stretched out in a different place on the carpet. I watched the late afternoon sun highlight the beautiful colors in her tortoiseshell coat, and I realized why she kept changing positions. She was following the sunlight. Each area she had chosen received a few hours of sunlight. She could rest in the warm glow all day.

I was struck with a spiritual application. Was I following the Son of God as closely as she followed the sunlight? When I stick close to Jesus, he provides comfort and warmth. But am I making the same kind of effort as my cat?

I'm not always aware of my spiritual surroundings. I miss out on living in the full light of Jesus' love and care if I'm not paying attention. Next time I find myself cold and alone, instead of complaining, I'm going to head to a patch of Son-light and curl up in perfect peace.

Dear God, you offer such comfort and peace. Why do I forget to stay close to you? Help me to follow your light. Sometimes, this world is a cold and dark place. Only when you illuminate my life am I truly at peace. You are the only one who can give me everything I need. Don't let me wander away from the light of your love. Instead, call me back to your side and keep me safe.

PAWS TO THINK

What are some of the ways the warmth of God's love makes life better?

DID YOU KNOW

On average, cats spend two-thirds of every day sleeping. That means a nine-year-old cat has been awake for only three years of its life.

WITH US

"Be strong and courageous.
Do not be afraid or terrified because of them,
for the LORD your God goes with you;
he will never leave you nor forsake you."

DEUTERONOMY 31:6 NIV

My husband's father had been in the VA for several months, and we had hoped for news that he was turning a corner and getting better. Instead, we were greeted with news no child wants to hear. It was time to call hospice and make some end of life decisions.

Saying goodbye to a parent is never easy. It was particularly hard with my husband's father. We lived several states away and couldn't be with him during the process.

We agonized over whether to move him to the hospice wing of the VA or move him to another facility. To start the process, a social worker took us downstairs to tour the hospice wing in the VA. As we got off the elevator, we were met with soft music and cheerful colors.

There were several rooms where veterans could gather,

as well as a tiny chapel. On the way to the rooms hallway, we met the only permanent resident—Wilson the cat. He was lounging in a chair, and as we walked by, he joined us for the tour. The social worker explained that the cat had been there several years and was a great favorite with residents and visitors.

Wilson had a knack for knowing who needed extra attention, and when it came time for a resident to say goodbye to this world, he made sure they never faced that transition alone. Our decision to leave my husband's father there brought us peace.

The call we dreaded came late one evening, but so did God's comfort. The nurse was quick to assure us that Wilson had stayed by Claude's side the entire day. It had been our greatest worry that he would be alone when he passed. God knew our fears, and he took care of them. I'm always amazed by the great lengths and creative methods God uses to answer prayers and bless his children.

God never falls short of his promises, and he promised to never leave us or forsake us. In this instance, he used a feline to fulfill his promise.

God, you are our comfort and our peace. You are always close when we need you. Remind me that your promises hold true for my loved ones as well as for me. It's harder to see the struggles of someone I care about than it is to face challenges myself. Give me real examples of the ways you care for those I love. Surround them with love. May I always trust your ability to be exactly what we need, when we need it.

PAWS TO THINK

How has God comforted you during times of stress and sorrow?

DID YOU KNOW

Cats can reduce blood pressure in patients while also reducing their fear and anxiety.

LOVING THE UNLOVABLE

*"If you love only those who love you,
why should you get credit for that?
Even sinners love those who love them!"*

LUKE 6:32 NLT

I watched as Emily slipped into the kitchen and studied my visitor. My friend had warned me she wasn't a cat person. I wasn't worried because my cat wasn't generally a people person. Emily wasn't interested in becoming friends with many people.

My friend and I grabbed our coffee and settled in my living room for a nice visit. My cat followed us into the room, and in that moment I knew the woman had been chosen to receive a precious—and unwelcome—gift.

Before I could intervene, Emily hopped up on the sofa between us. It was like a tiger had leapt on my friend. I lunged for my cat, caught her, and apologized to my friend.

Emily struggled, but I managed to get her upstairs and confine her to our bedroom. My friend had returned to the couch, this time perched on the edge, her eyes searching for the prowling cat. I assured her she wouldn't be back, and we finished our visit in peace.

Emily has continued to reach out to my friend, determined to make friends with the woman. Some would say Emily knew my friend didn't like her and was trying to torment her. But Emily's behavior hasn't been aggressive. Instead, she has gone out of her way to try to make friends.

God sometimes puts hostile people in my life. Some are angry people who erect defenses to keep others away. Others just don't like me. It's easier to ignore them, convincing myself I'm just doing what they want by leaving them alone.

Now, I'm rethinking my strategy. God expects us to love the unlovable and reach out to those who are hurting. I rarely show the kind of determination my cat did. These days, I am more persistent in trying to make friends with the scaredy-cats God has put in my life. If my cat can make an effort toward friendship, how can I do any less?

Dear God, you love me with an everlasting love. How can I refuse to show that love to all people I meet? When you first pursued me, I wasn't a very loveable person. I was downright hostile at times. Still, you kept after me, loving me during the worst moments of my life. How can I do any less for those you put in my path? When people are unfriendly, give me your immense patience. Keep me from turning my back on those who desperately need your love.

PAWS TO THINK

Who in your life is unlovable?
How can you reach out to them
and show God's love?

DID YOU KNOW

A cat lover is called an Ailurophilia.

RESIST TEMPTATION

"Watch and pray so that you will not fall into temptation.
The spirit is willing, but the flesh is weak."

MATTHEW 26:41 NIV

I was at my friend's house for an afternoon of coffee and conversation when our plans took a turn. We had just sat down at the kitchen table when my friend's yellow tabby cat walked in. She was coughing and wheezing.

My friend picked up her cat and inspected her. She was obviously in distress and getting worse by the second. I grabbed my keys. "I'll drive, and you can hold her," I said.

The receptionist looked up as we walked into the vet's office. Buttercup was wheezing even louder and still making little barking coughs. The woman took one look at the cat and called for a doctor.

My friend crooned encouragement to her pet and tried her best not to cry. The vet performed a cursory exam and informed us there was something lodged deep in the cat's throat. He took her into the back, promising to do his best.

At last, the vet returned. Buttercup would be fine. He

showed us a very damp and bedraggled piece of red ribbon, a tiny silver safety pin hanging from the end. She'd swallowed the ribbon, and the safety pin had caught in her throat. If we hadn't gotten help, she wouldn't have made it.

Temptation is a dangerous thing. It can lead to unwanted consequences we never imagined. Buttercup found that out the hard way. Buttercup couldn't pass up chewing on the ribbon, and it almost cost her life. I've also learned some hard lessons from giving in to things I shouldn't.

God promises to always provide a way out of temptation. He knows where our choices will lead, and he already has options in place to bring us safely through. I'm thankful that I also have a great physician who can put things right and get me back on track.

Dear God, I'm so weak sometimes. When something tempting beckons, I often run toward trouble without any thought for the consequences ahead. Help me to pause and take time to think before I act. Give me the wisdom I need to consider where my choices will lead me. I know that you always provide a way around the temptation, but it's not always easy to choose what's best. Surround me with friends who will help me make wise decisions instead of giving in to temptation.

PAWS TO THINK

Consider all the ways God provides before temptation strikes so you have a plan. What temptation do you often give in to?

DID YOU KNOW

The first cat in space was a French cat named Felicette (also known as "Astrocat"). In 1963, France blasted the cat into outer space. Electrodes implanted in her brain sent neurological signals back to earth. She survived the trip.

FACING GOLIATH

David triumphed over the Philistine
with only a sling and a stone, for he had no sword.

1 Samuel 17:50 nlt

I never thought of our timid cat taking on a dog seven times her size. She wasn't exactly a scaredy-cat, but she was more apt to run away than fight. That changed when our son and his wife adopted a precious—and active—puppy. Our older dog was less than thrilled with this boisterous baby, and our cat was downright hostile.

Brink was a puppy out to win anyone's heart. His urge to please and his happy spirit brought joy every time he visited. Even Jake warmed up to his canine cousin. The only one who refused to have anything to do with the new-comer was Emily.

At first, she disappeared up the stairs every time Brink rocketed into the house. As his visits became more fre-quent, she was less inclined to flee.

One day, she'd had enough. Instead of skulking at the top of our staircase, she went up three stairs and waited.

Sure enough, Brink came skidding around the corner and stopped. He stepped toward her, and she emitted a growling hiss that stopped him in his tracks. As he extended his nose, she glanced at me, then rose on her haunches and batted at his nose.

Without claws, she couldn't really hurt him, but her aggression caught him off-guard. He whined and backed away. This scenario repeated several times. He'd advance and she'd bop him on the nose. At the end of the lesson, it was obvious he accepted her as his superior, and she resumed her rightful place in our home.

God expects us to walk in the authority he's given us. When we are under God's protection, we have his strength and are supposed to use it—not hide in corners. Our focus must be on him not on the scary things that invade our lives.

Watching my cat face a giant adversary with no fear inspired me to take a look at the Goliaths in my life. If this delicate kitten could face down a massive dog with only me by her side, I could face my giants with confidence, knowing that God himself was fighting on my behalf.

God, many times I find myself afraid and fighting the urge to run and hide. I am overwhelmed by the giants that surround me. Remind me that I never fight alone. You are with me—not just to encourage me, but also to step into battle for me. You can take my small stature and bring about victories I never dared to imagine. Thank you for standing with me when I face my fears.

PAWS TO THINK

What are you afraid of right now?
Take those fears to God and let him
do the fighting for you.

DID YOU KNOW

Calico cats are almost always female.

ALWAYS ON TIME

The Lord is not slow about His promise, as some count slowness, but is patient toward you, not wishing for any to perish but for all to come to repentance.

2 Peter 3:9 NASB

Emma has always been a kittenish sort of cat—ready to play and pounce for no apparent reason. I'm certain Christmas is her favorite time of the year. I used to buy her cat toys at Christmas, but she virtually ignored them. There was always so much other loot to play with!

I can put up with the Christmas balls I find strewn across the floor, and the bits of tinsel that turn up in odd places. What I couldn't allow was Emma's love of climbing our Christmas tree. I didn't want her to get hurt, and I didn't want to lose my precious ornaments.

To deter her climbing, I invested in a squirt bottle. After a few douses from the bottle, she decided that climbing the tree wasn't all that tempting.

Then one evening, she came at the tree at a dead run, leaping into its uppermost branches before I could act.

Inevitably the tree toppled toward the ground. At the last possible moment, my husband came in from the garage and caught the tree before catastrophe struck.

Emma yowled and ran up the stairs. I don't know if she was scared or angry, but the lesson stuck. To this day, she's never tried to climb the tree.

I'm more like my cat than I like to admit. God gives me rules to follow—rules that will keep me from harm. However, the stuff I'm supposed to stay away from often seems harmless, a beautiful addition to add to my life. When I'm overcome with the urge to follow my own wants, I find myself in big trouble.

God is right there. He's always on time with the help I need, even when I'm the one who's gotten myself into a jam. He's on hand to catch me before I fall and set everything back in place. He'll do the same for you.

Dear God, why do I hesitate to come to you and ask for help? I always feel so ashamed, especially when the mess I'm in is from my own failures. I need to remember that you're always there to catch me when I fall. Your forgiveness and grace know no bounds. You're as quick to save me from myself as from any other predicament. Don't let me run from your help when I should be running toward it. You have proven your trustworthiness over and over. You are all I ever need.

PAWS TO THINK

When was the last time God showed up to rescue you just in the nick of time?

DID YOU KNOW

Approximately one-third of cat owners think their pets are able to read their minds.

WORK FOR US

"For I know the plans that I have for you" declares the LORD, "plans
for welfare and not for calamity to give you a future and a hope."

JEREMIAH 29:11 NASB

It was a desperate situation. A litter of tiny kittens had
been brought into the shelter when the mama cat was hit
by a car. These furry babies needed a lot of care, and there
weren't enough volunteers to care for them along with the
rest of the animals already housed there.

One enterprising volunteer came up with a possible solution. Her grandmother was a resident of a local
assisted living facility and was heartbroken because her
cat had recently passed away. The volunteer called the
manager and asked if her grandmother could help them
care for these kittens.

Not only was she able to help with their care, several
other residents also offered to help. The volunteer took the
kittens to their new foster home.

The women were at the door when the fosterlings
arrived. There were two kittens for each woman. The

volunteer explained how to feed the infants while they got to know their new charges. The kittens were so tiny; their eyes weren't even open. Still, they nestled in the laps of these loving women, at home and at peace.

It was the perfect solution to an almost impossible problem. The kittens received all the hands-on care they needed, and the residents felt a sense of purpose. The women have continued to work with the animal shelter, helping animals who need extra love and care.

No matter what stage of life we're in, God always has a plan. He used those tiny kittens to bring comfort and purpose to the residents. The residents were able to provide care that kept the kittens alive.

God is never done with us. He calls each of us to minister to a dark world. Sometimes that ministry looks big, at other times, it seems too small to matter. To God, there is never any big or small. What matters is our willingness to join him in his work.

Dear God, there are times when I feel useless. I think that you are done with me until you step in and call me to something new. Please don't let me take for granted the purpose you give my life. It's easy to feel good about the bigger things you ask me to do. I often forget that it's obedience you value most of all. Help me to recognize your call and be quick to say yes. You give my life purpose and joy. I wouldn't trade that for anything in the world.

PAWS TO THINK

Stop and consider all you're doing right now. Thank God for how he is using you to impact those around you.

DID YOU KNOW

A group of cats is called a clowder.

SOURCES FOR FUN FACTS

Page 6   buzzfeed.com/chelseamarshall/meows
Page 9   factretriever.com/cat-facts
Page 12   care.com/c/stories/6045/101-amazing-cat-facts-fun-trivia-about-your-feline-friend
Page 15   aspca.org/animal-homelessness/shelter-intake-and-surrender/pet-statistics
Page 18   catster.com/lifestyle/cat-whiskers-7-facts
Page 21   alleycat.org/resources/feral-and-stray-cats-an-important-difference
Page 24   factretriever.com/cat-facts
Page 27   petplace.com/article/cats/pet-behavior-training/why-do-cats-climb-trees
Page 30   buzzfeed.com/chelseamarshall/meows
Page 33   vetstreet.com/our-pet-experts/why-does-my-cat-hiss
Page 36   morningchores.com/barn-cats
Page 39   animalplanet.com/pets/why-do-cats-land-on-their-feet
Page 42   tripsavvy.com/rome-cats-sanctuary-amongst-the-ruins-of-rome
Page 45   quora.com/Why-are-cats-afraid-of-cucumbers
Page 48   guinnessworldrecords.com/world-records/largest-litter-domestic-cat
Page 51   catsinternational.org/amazing-cat-facts
Page 54   buzzfeed.com/chelseamarshall/meows
Page 57   petguide.com/blog/cat/how-to-calm-a-hyper-kitten/
Page 60   cattime.com/cat-facts/lifestyle/2022-top-10-cats-who-love-water
Page 63   cattime.com/cat-facts/health/189-amazing-cat-facts
Page 66   buzzfeed.com/chelseamarshall/meows
Page 69   buzzfeed.com/chelseamarshall/meows
Page 72   purina.com.au/cats/care/facts
Page 75   purina.com.au/cats/care/facts
Page 78   purina.com.au/cats/care/facts
Page 81   factretriever.com/cat.
Page 84   tractive.com/blog/en/safety/cat-sense-direction-explained
Page 87   factretriever.com/cat-facts
Page 90   kiddingkid.com/18-funny-interesting-cat-facts
Page 93   purina.com.au/cats/care/facts
Page 96   care.com/c/stories/6045/101-amazing-cat-facts-fun-trivia-about-your-feline-friend
Page 99   care.com/c/stories/6045/101-amazing-cat-facts-fun-trivia-about-your-feline-friend
Page 102   care.com/c/stories/6045/101-amazing-cat-facts-fun-trivia-about-your-feline-friend
Page 105   buzzfeed.com/chelseamarshall/meows
Page 108   buzzfeed.com/chelseamarshall/meows
Page 111   buzzfeed.com/chelseamarshall/meows
Page 114   buzzfeed.com/chelseamarshall/meows
Page 117   buzzfeed.com/chelseamarshall/meows
Page 120   buzzfeed.com/chelseamarshall/meows
Page 123   buzzfeed.com/chelseamarshall/meows
Page 126   care.com/c/stories/6045/101
Page 129   care.com/c/stories/6045/101-amazing-cat-facts-fun-trivia-about-your-feline-friend
Page 132   factretriever.com/cat-facts
Page 135   karmacatzendog.org/2016/07/29/15-things-didnt-know-cats
Page 138   karmacatzendog.org/2016/07/29/15-things-didnt-know-cats
Page 141   factretriever.com/cat-facts
Page 144   thedodo.com/cat-comforts-dying-vets-810505355.html
Page 147   factretriever.com/cat-facts
Page 150   factretriever.com/cat-facts
Page 153   catster.com/lifestyle/calico-cat-cats-are-awesome
Page 156   factretriever.com/cat-facts
Page 159   factretriever.com/cat-facts